Brooks Range
Passage

Brooks Range Passage

DAVID J. COOPER

THE MOUNTAINEERS
SEATTLE

THE MOUNTAINEERS: Organized 1906
"... to explore, study, preserve, and enjoy
the natural beauty of the Northwest."

Published by The Mountaineers
715 Pike Street, Seattle, Washington 98101

Published simultaneously in Canada by Douglas & McIntyre, Ltd.
1615 Venables Street, Vancouver, British Columbia V5L 2H1

Edited by Betsy Rupp Fulwiler
Book design by Elizabeth Watson
Typesetting by The Typeworks
Illustrations by Kurt D. Hollomon
Manufactured in the United States of America

Library of Congress Cataloging in Publication Data

Cooper, David J.
  Brooks Range passage.

  Bibliography: p.
  1. Brooks Range (Alaska)—Description and travel.
  2. Hiking—Alaska—Brooks Range. 3. Cooper, David J.
  I. Title.
F912.B75C66   1982   917.98′7   82-8194
ISBN 0-89886-061-X

To my father,
who showed me the beauty
and diversity of nature
and to my mother,
who gave me the courage
to create.

Contents

Acknowledgments

A book is always the work of many people, not just the author. This is true with this book, and I want to thank several people who helped at some stage. Bob Haynes and Chris and Shar White of Homer, Alaska, helped with planning the trip. Jerry Keenan and Evelyn Cooper encouraged me in writing the first draft. Dr. John Marr of the University of Colorado encouraged me to incorporate writing into my graduate studies. Barbara Steiner, Constance Brown, and Edward and Anita Cooper provided critical readings of the manuscript and gave helpful suggestions. Betsy Rupp Fulwiler as editor understood exactly what I was trying to achieve. Finally, and most importantly, I want to thank my entire family, who know how to worry just enough.

Preface

Brooks Range Passage is my journal of an experience that changed my life: a thirty-six-day solo trek through one of the most remote and beautiful wilderness areas remaining on earth, the Brooks Range in northern Alaska. Lying entirely north of the Arctic Circle and trending east-west across almost the whole state, it effectively forms a barrier between the boreal coniferous forests to the south and the arctic tundra to the north of the range. Glaciers of past eras have carved deep valleys rimmed with spectacular mountain peaks and ridges, creating a rugged territory that has not been hospitable to man.

From the Eskimo village of Anaktuvuk Pass, I hiked 120 miles through this rugged mountain terrain to the Arrigetch Peaks, the most dramatic cluster of pinnacles in North America. After building a log raft, I floated 160 miles down the Alatna River to where it meets the Koyukuk River at the Athabascan Indian village of Allakaket. During this journey, I experienced unimaginable frustrations and joys and learned that real wilderness does still exist. I also saw the great, pressing need to protect forever this irreplaceable avenue for human experience, which fast is being encroached upon by modern man and his real and imagined needs.

Wilderness is the pure expression of earth—the land, plants, animals, and interactions. It is possible to see entire ecosystems only in wilderness areas because only there are all the system's parts still present and functioning. In other areas man can merely guess or hypothesize about what they once were like. After my experience in the Brooks Range, I decided that ecological studies needed to be done there and I wanted to be part of the effort. I went back to college, pursuing graduate studies in ecology, and began fieldwork. I chose to begin my research in one valley in the range, so I could focus on the detailed interactions of the organisms and environment. I so far have spent three summers and a portion of one winter studying with companions in the Arrigetch Creek valley and the surrounding region. The area is experiencing a dramatic increase in visitor use, and a biological and ecological inventory and understanding are essential before the resources can be understood.

Biological studies are only a part of the efforts to preserve wild environments, however. A major role is played by people who make others aware of how important these lands are and how precarious their continued existence is. With this in mind, I set about getting the journal of my initial Brooks Range journey published, hoping that it could communicate not only the experience itself, but also the great joys and understanding that such lands can bring to man. However, in making the journal widely available, I did not intend to promote the journey as one that just anyone should undertake. It demands a great deal of preparation and knowledge of the area, not the least of which is a thorough understanding of the plants if one intends to eat them. For those who can benefit from such information, edible and poisonous plants mentioned in my journal are noted by both their Latin and common names to avoid any dangerous confusion as to their identity. Common names are given in other cases where knowing the exact technical names is not essential.

Most human experiences will not occur in remote areas such as the Brooks Range. But it is very important for us to seek out undisturbed quiet segments of our environment in order to feel the incredible simplicity and wonderment of earth as well as the difficulties and suffering that such encounters inevitably bring. We need to allow our minds and senses to be open and atuned to the natural world around us, for it is as real and provides as much meaning as our man-made world.

Five hundred years ago on this continent, man lived in wilderness. What will it be like fifty or five hundred years from now? Our undisturbed lands are shrinking rapidly as our resource needs increase. Simultaneously, the need to experience undisturbed lands is increasing rapidly as the human population grows. The globe is not infinite. We must have room to experience wild lands on this planet, for they are a vital tie to our ancestry and heritage besides being a vital need of our minds and bodies.

Introduction

During my travels in wilderness areas in the lower forty-eight states, I had always wondered what the country was like two hundred years ago, before such things as trails, roads, and ski areas. I went to Alaska to find an immense undeveloped region where I could see and experience virgin country. I thought that such contrasts would clarify my perception of how our modern domestic culture has changed wild lands and how it determines what experiences are available to most people and to me. Having heard about how the trans-Alaska pipeline was opening up country such as the Brooks Range that most human beings have never seen, I wanted to experience the country while it was still primitive.

I spent the winter of 1976 in Homer, Alaska, engaged in commercial crab fishing in Kachemak Bay. All the while I played with the idea of spending the coming summer hiking across the Brooks Range. I studied maps of the area for several months to familiarize myself with the character of the mountains and valleys, and I discussed my ideas with several friends in Homer. I sought companions, but without success. I was not trying to tempt fate, but I thought it was better to go alone than to choose a wrong companion. I became interested in the Endicott Mountains, the area drained by the Koyukuk River on the south and the Colville River on the north. They looked immense, rugged, and undisturbed, and had been proposed as the Gates of the Arctic National Park. (The area officially became a national monument in 1979.)

I chose to start at Anaktuvuk Pass at the northern edge of the mountains, and head west and south in a zigzagging route, following valleys and crossing divides in remote country that I had seen only in a few photographs. I chose to end my journey at Allakaket or Kobuk, the closest villages to the southwest, and a distance of three hundred miles. Traveling between villages seemed most feasible because the villages were located at prominent crossroads in the great expanse of country. They would be relatively easy to find and have frequent, inexpensive transportation (at least by Alaska standards). The idea of waiting for someone to pick me up and having to meet a schedule in order to be at a certain place by a certain time, and then waiting if I was early, would have taken much of the spontaneity out of the journey. I wanted to be totally free to move as I pleased without any concept of time, except how many more weeks my food supply would last.

Because there would be no food drops and no rendezvous, I had to have everything at the start that I would need to complete my trip. As soon as I left the village at Anaktuvuk Pass, I would be on my own. Rescue would be out of the question, because of the vastness of the area. I had studied botany and ecology in college, and I went through Eric Hulten's *Flora of Alaska and Neighboring Territories* cover to cover many, many times to become thoroughly familiar with the plants that I would see. I memorized every species that had potential as a food source, because I knew I would have to supplement my diet daily in order to keep myself healthy and adequately fed. After many weeks of thinking, I decided on a minimum daily ration of dry foods: a third cup each of cornmeal, whole wheat flour, and a mixture of brown rice, barley, and lentils, plus a half cup of granola oat cereal. I would carry enough basic foodstuffs for six weeks—a total of fourteen cups each of cornmeal, wheat flour, and the rice mixture, ten pounds of granola, a few cups of split peas and beans, four pounds of honey, five pounds of peanuts, a few pounds of powdered milk, a pound of brown sugar, two pounds of raisins, and two pounds of other dried fruit. Fats would be most precious; I carried three pounds of margarine and two pounds of lard. A small amount of baking powder, a few pounds of cheese, and some bread to help me through the first couple of days rounded out my dietary provisions. The rest I would have to harvest from the land and water of the mountains.

When July 1 arrived, Bob Haynes, who was skipper of the

boat on which I fished, took me to the Homer airport. My pack didn't seem very heavy, yet I still had many items to add. I carried my camera equipment and film over my shoulder. When I put the pack on the scales, the lady weighing luggage looked up at me and said, "Where do you think you're going?" It weighed ninety-six pounds! My heart fell, because I knew it would go well over a hundred pounds by the time I reached Anaktuvuk Pass.

I flew from Homer to Anchorage, took the Alaskan Railway to Fairbanks, then flew to Bettles. The mail plane was supposed to fly on to Anaktuvuk soon afterward, but an early summer snowstorm was whitening the Brooks Range, and the flight was delayed. While I waited, I started talking with some of the Bettles locals. One man had seen my bow and arrows and asked whether I had anything to back them up. I smiled, not really knowing what he meant, and said no. He smiled back and proceeded to describe how last spring he had been hiking, and for some reason, he had taken his rifle (he rarely does so). Along the river he came up over a rise, and there in a clearing ahead he saw some antlers sticking up and a large brown mound next to them. He stopped short, and as he did, the brown thing raised its head and charged. The grizzly bear had been feeding on a caribou carcass. The man emptied his rifle into the hulking body, and it died at his feet.

My face became distorted and my eyes went far away. Visions of grizzly bears chasing me over the ridge and into the sunset filled my mind, and my feet got cold. It was hours before I even partially recovered. I had thought about bears many times. You can't help it living in Alaska. Before leaving Homer, I had developed two trends of thought, wrestling with both of them off and on. One was that I didn't want to die, not for anything. There was too much to live for, and I would defend my life as man has always done. The other philosophy was that this is wild country; it belongs to the wild creatures who live here. Who am I to enter this land and kill them if they should threaten me? Visitors who kill the large wild mammals will destroy those animal populations and the wilderness that

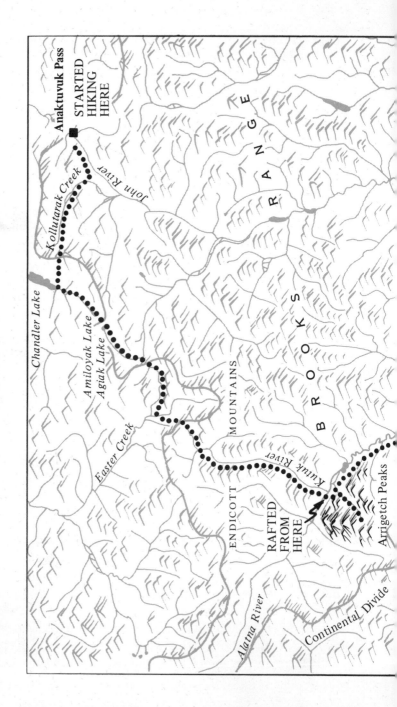

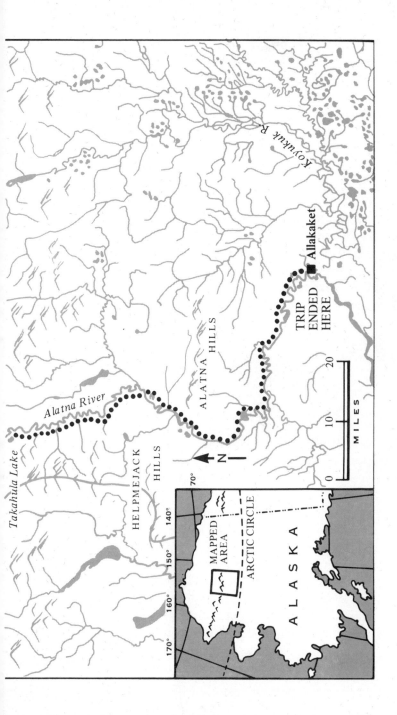

they represent. I left Homer intending to travel unprotected by firearms.

I also met two young Eskimo women from Anaktuvuk Pass. I told them what I was going to do. One warned me that I was foolish, that I would get lost and die, or drown crossing a river or be destroyed by a bear, or experience some other fatal end. After these two episodes, I became hesitant to tell my plans to anyone else in town.

Later that day, after conversing with many people, I happened to talk with a pilot who was flying two National Park Service people around the Central Brooks Range. They were reviewing the landscape for potential boundaries for the proposed Gates of the Arctic National Park. I told him I had come to do some hiking in that area, and he suggested that I talk with the two men. The next morning, Ray Bane and John Kauffmann found me, and I laid out my entire plan for them, using maps to trace my planned route. They listened without speaking, then pointed out places they had visited. They had flown over much of the proposed national park area and told me about the valleys they considered impassable by foot. Ray also told me how the Kobuk River Eskimo built large rafts to float down the rivers that flow south from the Brooks Range. He described the design and which rivers he thought would be navigable by this primitive method.

They knew nothing of wild edibles, and the pilot further discouraged me by saying the mountains looked barren and sparsely vegetated. He did not think I could find "anything to eat down there." John and Ray were calm, however, and more experienced. They knew the natives had used many indigenous plants for their subsistence. I planned only to visit the Brooks Range, not remain there, although winters are separated by a very short interlude of summer. I had to be prepared to survive the experience and not get trapped by an early winter. A person's mind always butts up against thoughts like these when he goes into new country and is not sure what will happen, how long things will take, and what will be possible or impossible. He finds out only as each day unfolds, and then he must make continual adaptations.

The day for starting my trek across the Brooks Range came soon enough. I remember talking to one native woman as the plane was being loaded. I asked her how the blueberries in the area were. She laughed and said she still had five gallons left from last summer. We talked of the old days. She remembered that when she was a young girl, Robert Marshall, who in the 1930s was the first nonnative to see parts of the Central Brooks Range, had spent time around Bettles. The memories of the old ways and the old land came back to her easily. Why is it that thoughts of wilderness and frontiers stir up such romantic images within us? Is it the wild country itself we feel so strongly about because of some innate bond we have within us? Is it the people we imagine are living there? Or do we respond to what we think we will feel and how alive and acute our senses will become in wilderness? I wasn't sure, but I was following my own urges to see this country, to experience myself, to live in and with the Brooks Range, one of the last segments of North American wilderness.

PART ONE

Walking

July 6

As the little Cessna streaks down the gravel runway and arches toward the heavens, I take my first, long look at the sky: gray clouds huddle in masses against the mountains, dissected in spots by piquant blue. As we level off over the John River, which will guide us through the mountains to Anaktuvuk Pass, I press my nose to the window to get a view of the earth below. The John meanders in numerous bends, some almost complete circles, as it flows toward the ocean. Hills south of the Brooks Range form a gentle terrain of forested uplands and boggy lowlands. Tiny streams snake every which way around hills and islands of trees, and disappear into patches of standing water. These wetlands support the most striking array of color in natural vegetation that I have ever seen. Black spruce with an understory of whitish lichens give way to bright green shrubby birches and willows, which change to golden sedges and mosses as the water deepens. The landscape is infinitely colorful and varied as I look from the river to the bogs and hills and up to the approaching Brooks Range, which we soon enter. The John River valley is broad with old river terraces, the remnant flood plains from when the river flowed at higher levels in the valley.

Strips of forest run up the valley, keeping to higher, well-drained ground. The mountains are not like those in southern Alaska, where huge glaciers fill the valleys. Snowfall here is not great enough to produce glaciers, and valleys are broad, graceful U's with a veneer of light green vegetation. The valley sides are steep, rising to cliffs and broken summits. The country seems smooth and polished. I stare from the droning aircraft's window up each new valley and am transfixed by the undisturbed flowing qualities of each one. Alluvial fans, formed by sediments being washed by rain down slopes and deposited at the mountain's base, pour from every break in the valley walls, and spread their broadening forms into the bottomlands. Streams that seem whitened with their rushing are fed by high pockets of lingering winter snow and a thin coat of glimmering white from the past weeks' storms. Trees become sparse on the valley sides as we continue north, being replaced by a heavy, shrubby growth. The river starts to straighten, and the spruce trees linger on only the old stream terraces. Even these thin out into islands of trees, then individuals, and finally are left behind entirely.

The valley bends sharply to the northeast, and soon I see some individual mountains that I have previously noted in photographs. I recognize that we must be approaching Anaktuvuk Pass. Then we descend from our mountaintop elevation and pass over the village. It doesn't seem quite real, this tiny, permanent outpost in the middle of a great mountain range. Isolated from all but themselves and the mountains, the inhabitants surely must love it here or they could never stay. I know that by the 1970s, most Alaska natives have traveled to Fairbanks and other nonnatives' towns. Some even occasionally go "outside" to the "lower forty-eight," but most still come back to live in their village with their people.

We fly in a great circle toward Soakpak Mountain to the northwest, and back around to Anaktuvuk. I can see what must be the runway, but it's just a large scratch in the tundra, as if a huge hand with claws had reached out and stirred up the dirt a bit. The plane slows, touches down, jostles, and bumps around, blurring my vision, but it lands intact. At the end of the runway, we turn and taxi back to the village where a crowd is already gathering. The mail plane with cargo and other supplies comes in only twice a week. The people gather around the plane, and I feel as if I have been drugged. Am I really ready for this?

The doors are opened, and the townspeople start to unload the cargo. I step out and the mosquitoes rush in. I sweep my hand in front of my face and then put the insects out of my mind. These people are Nunamaiut, a tribe of Eskimo whose name means "caribou people." The caribou traditionally provides the majority of their food and clothing. They are now dressed in down jackets and nylon parkas except for one old fellow who buzzes around the plane on a snowmobile. He wears a caribou parka and mukluks, and his bronze face supports a triumphant smile that shows few teeth. He stops momentarily. Boxes are loaded onto his machine, and he ferries them across the tundra into the village. He obviously enjoys his work and makes numerous zigzags just for fun. He sees me take my hunting bow from the plane and pulls up alongside me. Holding out his left hand he concentrates, then slowly says, "Choom? Zing?" Then he throws his hand up in the air and we both laugh. He obviously doesn't speak much English, but no words are needed. In almost all remote villages in Alaska, there are a few elderly people who have lived most of their lives without the modern conveniences that now pervade their society. These people give the real flavor—or at least the flavor most nonnatives imagine—to these villages, because Eskimo are usually still thought of as primitive even though they are, in most respects, as modern as other North American inhabitants.

The pilot helps me carry my pack from the plane, and we set it down on the ground with my bow on top of it. A man in a red parka asks me where I am going and I remember the answer of the two girls in Bettles. I say I am going to Chandler Lake and ask how the fishing is. He says there are trout in the lake and grayling in the streams. The village people travel there in winter and spring by snowmobile or airplane to fish through the ice. Another man sees my bow and points to it saying, "Watch out for bears. But if you see one, bring him back here. We'll eat him for you." They all get a big laugh out of it. But recalling the story at the Bettles airport, I fail to appreciate the humor.

Finally, the Nunamaiut people return to the village. The pilot shakes my hand and we say good-bye. He climbs in his plane and flies off. It takes me a while to get everything secured, then I try to lift my pack. I cannot lift it onto my shoulder or even a knee. I must sit beside it, slip into the shoulder straps, and bend over so its weight is on my back. Then I get on all fours and work my way to a kneeling position. From there, it's all leg muscle to try to stand upright. After a struggle, it is settled on my back, in the way it will sit for many days to come. It weighs between 100 and 110 pounds and the thought of carrying "the thing," makes me ill. But I do what one must do in circumstances like this: I put it out of my mind and wobble on into the village.

Most of the dwellings are relatively modern wood cabins and frame homes. One old sod hut stands in the middle of the other buildings, and dates back to the years before there was a permanent village here. I have talked with several nonnatives who have told me of spending time with these same people in the early 1940s along the eastern shore of Chandler Lake. They would stay in one place as long as the caribou kept migrating through that valley. When the caribou changed their migration route to another valley, the people followed them. A permanent village was established in the late 1940s by United States government order, so children could go to school at Anaktuvuk Pass where the natives had settled at the time.

People sit on their porches or in their backyards, and children run in the dirt lanes between the homes. I walk slowly, trying to get a feel for summer life in the village. Little is going on, and no one approaches me as I head for the hill that leads toward the south and the mouth of the Kollutarak River.

Starting up the slope, I feel my body groaning under the weight of the pack that I had "put out of my mind." I search for another diversion from this pain and am at once surrounded by the brightness of summer blossoms. My eyes beam, my steps end, and I scan the meadow that greets my entry into the Brooks Range. Mountain avens stretch out all over the hillslope and thousands of white-petaled blossoms dance in the gentle breeze of midday. Lapland rosebay and arctic bell heather mingle among the mountain avens. These strange wild blossoms awaken in me the feeling of how rare and beautiful this country is. I want to put my hands to the earth and lift a tuft of the dangling heather bells to my shoulder so that it may take root there and travel the Brooks Range with me. But the middle of a hill is a bad place to stop walking, as it makes starting too difficult. I direct my senses toward the top of the rise, controlling my mind that wants to play with the delicate flowers and my body that wants relief from this first encounter with the rigors of the trip, and march to the top.

At the crest, I set my load on the ground and spend some time enjoying the display. I think to myself, "If it all is like this, my time will be filled with infinite beauty." I also know that I will make very few miles this day.

The landscape is dissected by many small gullies and depressions, which act as small snow-accumulation areas, thus changing the environmental conditions of temperature, moisture, and winter snow cover (which some of the windier sites lack) for these microhabitats. In the more moist habitats different plants grow, such as tall willow, dwarf birch, Labrador tea, and the most showy species of all, arctic poppy. This poppy stirs the imagination. How does such a slender stem support such a well-developed blossom without yielding to gravity?

This layer of dwarf vegetation on these rolling hills is lovely, but I see that the peak bloom has already passed and the site's dry character is showing through. Petals are falling, seed pods lay exposed to the sun, and though it is only the first week in July, summer is well under way. I hoist the load to my back and set off across the tundra. The turf has been firm and the walking pleasant up until now, but as I walk on across the terrace, I hit a field of cotton grass tussocks. They are shaped like a vertical cylinder, and grow larger around than a basketball and twelve to eighteen inches high. They are the product of myriad years' accumulation of dead growth from leaves and stems of the cotton grass, which builds vertically to form them. Usually there are several inches of space between tussocks—just enough room for one thin foot. Walking on top of them seems like the best way of negotiating this type of country. Unfortunately, they do not support my weight, and as they bend, I plummet to the earth. Sprawled on the lumpy ground, I reach to the bottom of one of the gaps between them and realize that there is an inch or more of standing water and mud there. The idea of wet feet makes me seek higher ground, zigzagging across the valley looking for terrain that does not have tussocks. The only alternatives are high on the mountain or in the river.

Most of the Brooks Range is underlaid with permanently frozen ground called permafrost. The summer heat thaws the ground a few inches or a few feet, but below that it stays frozen. Early in the summer, snowmelt from winter's accumulation cannot permeate the soil to any depth, and the ground becomes saturated, causing the water to run off the surface or pool up. In areas of flat or gentle terrain, such as broad valley bottoms and terraces, water lingers and produces the soggy ground with which I am confronted. Vertical growth of these tussocks must be a beneficial growth form, for they are very successful here. People had told me that much of northern Alaska is tussock country, but I had not anticipated the seemingly endless expanses of it in the Brooks Range.

One problem with tussocks is that I constantly am lifting up my legs and watching the ground so I can position my feet with each step. This way I don't slip, but I tire every hundred yards or so and want to sit down. There are few rocks and high, dry spots and the flexible tussocks bend under my weight. I find it important not to take off the pack, because putting it on again is too difficult. I relieve the weight of the pack by resting its bottom upon a couple of close-growing large tussocks, and then I semi-sit and lie back upon my pack to provide needed relief. After about a mile of this, I begin to get panicky, thinking if "tussocking" is going to be like this, hiking is going to be hard work, I will have to look for enjoyment on the side, when I rest or stop.

Tussock tundra forces me to focus on the ground so I can choose a path through the maze of mounds. At times, I can't help getting down on my knees to look at all the microhabitats. In some places, Labrador tea and alpine blueberry (*Vaccinium uliginosum*) grow along the margins of the tussocks, and the sides support luxuriant leaflike lichens and mats of moss. Each tussock is slightly different in shape and size, and in the variety and abundance of its inhabitants. The potential for enjoying this remarkable vegetation is almost infinite for a naturalist, but the potential for it to make movement miserable also is constantly present, defying my body's ability to act as a machine and restricting my observations solely to its forms when I am walking.

It is a cool, cloudy afternoon. I have not noticed myself sweating, but I reach down to wipe some mud off my hand onto my T-shirt and notice that the shirt is totally soaked and sticking to my body. I sit down to take a long rest and a profusion of mosquitoes is attracted to me. I want to open my wool shirt to let my body cool off, but instead button it up. I don my head net and sit back to watch the insects. They certainly are different from others I have seen. It is not that they are any larger in size, but their approach is amazing. All the temperate zone mosquitoes I have dealt with in the Rocky Mountains gently light on my body without stirring up their landing area too much. These arctic counterparts take a run at it and dive, bouncing by the hundreds off my head net. The noise produced by their strikes sounds as if someone is pummeling me with tiny stones. It is a teeming display of aggression and determination, and provides me with great entertainment when I actually sit down to enjoy the striving little creatures. For walking, my net becomes an uncomfortable mask. Too much light is cut off, making the day even gloomier and confining. A double dose of bug juice is in order, and in the breeze of the afternoon, my bare face survives the onslaught of the hungry beasts.

One of the most important things to develop on a trip like this is a walking pace that allows good progress while not straining the body's capacity. The biggest danger is that the whole trip could become a grueling experience because of the rigors of primitive travel. Although these difficulties are encountered numerous times daily, they should not occupy my first thoughts when I wake in the morning. To set a pace, I must learn to control my body with a part of my brain that does not need conscious and constant urging. Then my conscious self can explore the country and be free to expose and evaluate my emotions. This is critical, for only if I am able to understand the experience and compare it with other experiences can I realize the effect the wild land is having upon me. Without this, my journey will not achieve one of its greatest purposes.

I walk parallel to the John River, and numerous gullies cross my path headed for the river. Tall willows grow along the sides of the gullies, reaching eight or ten feet in height. These are the only local source of sticks or wood, so I gather four straight but flimsy, two-foot poles to use as tent supports. Evening in the Brooks Range in early July comes when the sun slips northward and hides behind the mountains. I cannot see the sun but know that it must be getting close to that time as the sky is dimming. I head for a small rock outcrop where I hope to find dry ground. The ground is dry but far from flat and smooth. I lay down a piece of plastic and start to think of ways to make a shelter using my rain poncho. As the sky descends, I feel the moist chill of the breeze and know it will rain this evening. I take two of the poles, cross them about two inches from the top, and with a small piece of string, tie them together. I spread the bases about two and a half feet apart, and plunge them a few inches into the resistant turf. Then I take a piece of string perhaps twelve feet long, and tie a stake to each end. One stake I plant about two feet beyond the poles, then draw the string over the poles and plant the other stake when the string is taut. I drape my poncho over this and put rocks at the corners and intermittently along the sides to hold it taut. I then put my dense foam pad and my sleeping bag inside, and my sleeping quarters are ready. I don't feel like cooking as the day had been too late in starting, so I have a meager dinner of cheese, bread, and a hard-boiled egg saved from my breakfast in Bettles. I prop my pack upright against a boulder and snugly cinch down the top so no rain can enter. How far I am from Bettles now!

The temperature is dropping rapidly and the mosquitoes leave the air. I crawl into my shelter, but it isn't high enough to sit up in so I undress on my side and slip into my bag. I zip it up as far as I can and lay my head on my down vest. The rain falls as a mist at first, moistening the earth. The wind rustles through the rocks and ripples my tent. I can tell the rocks aren't going to hold things taut, but I close my fatigued eyes as the drops drum against my shelter. Lulled, I sleep.

Tussocks

The "night" goes on in that strange way that nights do in unfamiliar places. I sleep, then awaken, then sleep, many times. The rain comes down in violent thrusts, ceases, then is replaced by intermittent wind. When the rain suddenly strikes the poncho, inches above my head, in a driving new burst of life, the suddenness and the closeness of the noise startle me from slumber. My eyes do not want to open, but I continually must check my shelter for stability and leaks. The sides of the poncho where rocks hold it to the ground are catching the runoff from the peak of the tent and the water is pooling there. The same thing is happening at the foot of the tent. My sleeping bag is in contact with these pools and is dampening. I roll over from my back to my side and curl as tightly as is comfortably possible in order to avoid the wet spots.

The ground is a maze of lumps. The sore spots in my back constantly remind me of the many hours of coping with these mounds of vegetation. On my side, I bend, trying to fit into a line of valleys between the mounds. It is far from comfortable, but the situation does not lend itself to much comfort. From a series of impossible positions I choose one of comparable bliss, and as the rain continues and the noise becomes familiar, I try to talk myself to sleep. The myriad problems already encountered are running through my brain, and visions of other unimaginable problems fight with the visions of beautiful miles to come. The tug-of-war pulls at my mind.

Now at the trip's onset, while still close to my starting point, I try to review all the reasons that have brought me to this mountain range, of all ranges on earth, and why I have come at this time in life, alone, and by primitive, unaided methods of travel. Faces appear and dissolve in my mind— people I love thousands of miles away, people I grew up with. How have I ever arrived at a place so far from where I used to run? Many people have never heard of the Brooks Range; few will ever care about it. What the hell am I trying to prove? What do I want to learn that is so important that I am risking my life for it in this strange odyssey?

I think of my scientific interest. I will be seeing and experiencing country in a way that few science-oriented observers ever have the chance to. I will be walking in valley after valley, and experiencing the change in vegetation from north to south, arctic to boreal. I will be living with the land and seeing it in its unmodified form. I will be eating native plants and animals and acquiring the knowledge of where to find them. I will be learning the country's forms so that, before heading toward an area, I can tell from the types of vegetation how hard the walking will be there. I will be looking for interesting features, plants, and animals to distract my brain from the rigors of walking. I will be becoming familiar with the big game living in the area, and though some species have been reduced considerably, I will be getting an idea of where the animals lived and will be able to hypothesize why they lived there. Besides this unique naturalistic education, I will be getting an anthropological education, seeing the land in terms of its potential to support human life and to provide comforts as well as routes for travel. I will be able to feel what it was like to live here as an Eskimo in primitive times, trying to make a living entirely from this land.

In the modern United States, the essentials of life—finding something to eat, not only for survival but also for contentment, water to drink, and wood to make fire for cooking, warmth, and drying—are taken for granted. Here, I have enough food for survival, but every day I will have to gather the bulk of my diet, all my water, and firewood. I will have to take care of myself starting with the basics, and once those are secured, other affairs such as walking, writing, and enjoying the country can be pursued. I will be as a primitive man, one without the company of other people, and I will discover for myself the innate urges that keep a being motivated to survive on his own power and will. These seem like steps taken by all our ancestors, possibly every day of their lives. I want to find out if these dormant instincts can be reawakened, and what it will feel like to provide for both my bodily needs and mental motivation.

I will have time to sort out my ideas of the modern working world and compare them with primitive life, recognizing the merits and shortcomings of each, and see if I can understand why man consistently progresses away from the primitive. I have to learn these things for myself, to see just where I belong. Should I shape my life around the modern or the primitive? Should I combine the two?

I am awakened by a gust of wind sending cold, damp air down my neck and back. It must be "morning"—the sky seems lighter. Clouds hang at the valley tops, covering the peaks and high ridges. Rain is intermittent and light. I lie dozing for some time, until I start to see a few patches of blue sky through the clouds. I tell myself the weather will break, and I dress for the day. My boots are still soggy, the leather spongy and slimy, but dry socks make them feel comfortable. A wool sweater and shirt are in order as the morning wind is sharp and blustery. My sleeping bag is wet through at the foot and along the sides. Glad it is filled with synthetic fibers that do not absorb water, I stuff it into a nylon bag. Then I stow my sleeping gear and shelter, and dig into my morning rations. I mix a measly third of a cup of granola with some raisins, powdered milk, and water, then eat quickly. My hunger hardly appeased, I finish the bread and cheese left over from yesterday and realize that I must consistently provide food for myself or hunger will be a constant companion.

I hoist my pack to my knee and work my arms into it. It is as heavy as ever, and I can tell it will probably lose weight more reluctantly than my body will. The wind is blowing strongly and steadily at about thirty miles per hour. I pull down the earflaps on my cap and start off toward the Kollutarak. The slope is steep and rocky, and I spend much time making short distances between ribbons of talus. The scattered patches of vegetation are composed of tough, cushion-like plants that make fine walking. I try to stay on the turf, winding my way among piles of boulders, but have to climb up and over many that block my path. A bald eagle soars by on the wind, and I think that he seems out of place in the Brooks Range, but apparently he can sustain himself on the fish in the John River.

I have spent a lot of time in windy country in the Rockies and have never really cared for the wind. Here the opposite is true, as it keeps the mosquitoes on the ground or on my lee side. The wind is blowing from the northwest, and there is a cloud of mosquitoes against and adjacent to the part of my body that faces southeast. If I rapidly change my body position or bend over, all the bugs are blown away from me or to the ground. It's so nice to sit back on a rock, face into the wind, and know that there's not a mosquito in sight.

I soon come to a bend in the John River valley, and get my first look at the Kollutarak. The valley is broad, very green, and looks deceptively smooth from my elevation on the mountainside. Another valley that runs almost parallel to the Kollutarak surrounds Masu Creek, which feeds into the Kollutarak, and these waters are supplemented by Ekokpuk Creek before all of their waters merge with that of the John River. A great open area results, with intergrading rivers and many small ponds scattered across the six or eight miles of rolling terrain. I stop to look back up the John toward Anaktuvuk Pass and the miles I have covered so far, and then down the long winding valley toward the southwest, where the valley bends sharply to the south; I can see no farther. Two semipalmated plovers run in front of me, cheeping at my presence, but continue untroubled across the dry tundra. I think the grand size of the valleys and open areas between the mountain ridges are the most striking features of this view. I can see only a few miles up the Kollutarak, as the valley makes a sharp bend to the west. It signals the first real channel that will lead me away from civilization, away from the airplane corridor of the John River, deep into the Brooks Range.

I stay high on the northern valley side, not wanting to lose my elevation until I can spot a reasonable route to follow.

Steep mountains rise on both sides of the valley, ending in cliffs and broken crags. The valley bottom is broad with that ever-deceiving smooth-flowing tundra character that seems to promise gentle terrain and easy walking. The mountainside is rocky, and I descend to a river terrace that beckons with its flat, dry character. From a distance, tussocks appear to blend into a seemingly homogeneous layer of vegetation, and it is only upon approaching them that they swell up from the ground to antagonize my feet and wear down my body. It becomes apparent that the tussocks are merely camouflaged by vertically and horizontally growing herbs and shrubs. Tussocks grow only in the poorly drained areas, but sometimes it seems as if the whole valley bottom fulfills that characteristic.

Resting among some tussocks that have a covering of shrubby birches, I am visited by savannah sparrows, which flit about among the shrubs and soon make their way toward some tall willows along the river. They are very common and unstriking birds. At any sitting, I can hear their sounds among the grasses and sedges. Equally common but more beautiful are the Lapland longspurs. With the chestnut patch at the back of the neck, golden eye stripe, and black throat and crown, the males are easily identified. Birds seem to be the only consistent form of animal life (except for insects), and I watch them as much as possible and cherish their companionship. Most of these birds winter thousands of miles south of here, in the continental United States and South America, and I acknowledge our common bond of spending this summer in these valleys.

The valley starts to bend westward, and I see large patches of ice along the river, which look like solid walking. This feature, called aufeis, forms in fall, winter, and spring, when a portion of the river freezes and water must flow over and around the ice. Water freezes atop and along it, increasing the thickness and causing more water to flow laterally onto the flood plain, where it also freezes. This ice builds up with periods of early or late winter melt. In times of moderate or heavy runoff, when silt and sand are carried by the stream, this too is moved over the ice, and some is frozen in, giving the ice a layered effect. In spring when the stream discharge increases, it cuts through the ice in the stream channel, but the ice on the flood plain lingers, melting as the season warms. If the deposits of ice are large enough, they may persist for the entire summer. Where the ice is cut sheer by the river, tongues of mud spill out from their storage home, between two heavy slabs. Walking on it is nice, although meltwater is pooled in places, and slush and water soak my boots. Against the gray, overcast sky, the blue of the ice shines dimly below the layers of whitening, melting slush. Branches poke through the ice, and I wonder whether they were deposited here by the river, or whether they are attached to some rooted streamside shrub. Surely, if this mass of ice forms here yearly, then no shrub would survive the consistent burial and shortened growing season.

Soon the ice ends and I step down onto a soggy sedge meadow tinged red with a moss that inhabits these ice marginal areas. Water is ankle-deep, and I head on tiptoes toward the rocky braided stream channel. Rocks are almost as bad for walking as tussocks when they are large, and I wind a path along the river. I look for patches of sand and gravel and follow them, occasionally leaping to river bars, taking advantage of whatever flat ground exists. Another patch of ice is ahead, but it is on the other side of the creek. I stop at some large rock, slip my pack off, take off my boots and socks, and put on my tennis shoes. I have drawstrings around the cuffs of my pants and pull them up to mid-thigh and cinch them. I hoist my pack and waddle toward the creek. Looking down, I find that the mosquitoes are having a field day on my legs. I run to the stream and splash them off with the first two steps. I brace myself and start across the stream, which is about fifty feet across, mid-thigh deep, and cold. By the time I get ten feet into the river my feet are numb. I rush across and quickly sit on the shore. My legs are spotted red and white like a shrimp and I take off my shoes to let my skin dry before putting on my boots again.

The sun is somewhere in the west, dipping constantly lower toward the north. I look for a spot to spend the evening and find a large, high lobe that is semidry on top with a space between some shrubs that looks large enough to sleep in. I drop my pack and lay out my ground cloth and sleeping bag to give them time to dry. I piece my fly rod together, tie a black-gnat dry fly on the end of the leader, and head down to the stream. There are many four- to five-foot willows growing along the stream meanders and pools. I cast my fly in below a riffle and then into a pool with large rocks. Nothing. A fish darts across the stream and into a large, deep, calm, almost stagnant pool. I flip out my gnat and catch a grayling. Wow! This is a good sign. I had hoped that I could depend upon grayling for a rich addition to my diet. The fish are only six to eight inches long, but there are many in the stream, so I take four. The grayling is very different from any fish I have seen, with a small puckered mouth and huge dorsal fin. I run happily across the bumpy tundra to my camp. Carrying a handful of dead willow branches to make a fire, I search around and gather three rocks to make a stand on which to put my pot. Then I order my kindling into a small tepee and set a match to it. I start a quart of water to boiling and add a pinch of salt and a third cup of my rice-barley mixture into which I add a small handful of lentils. Feeding four-inch pieces of willow to my fire, I watch the smoke rise and melt into the air.

When my brown rice is almost finished cooking, I put the gutted grayling into the pot. They cook a few minutes, and I stir them into the soup as they break apart. Their fat spots the surface of the soup, and I add a spoonful of margarine to it. A large volume of water is used to act as a filler-upper. I dig in as soon as it is ready and immediately learn something. Having eaten trout and similar freshwater fish for so many years, I did not consider that grayling would have large scales. My meal is accompanied with continual spitting. It is quite satisfying, however, to feel the warmth and weight of the meal in my stomach. Before my fire dies, I mix a third cup each of cornmeal and whole wheat flour in my measuring cup, then add some raisins, a dab of baking powder, and enough water to get it all wet but not runny. I heat my frying pan, lightly grease it with a bit of lard, and spoon the mixture on. After frying it on both sides, I end up with four biscuits, each about two inches across. I then cool them and put them in a plastic sack for lunch tomorrow.

It is evening, and the sky is clear. The wind slows down and settles into a calm. All day, the mountains to the north have been covered with a wind cloud, formed as air moves from a valley, over a mountain ridge, and back down into another valley. It is wavelike motion, and as the air rises to crest the ridge, it cools, moisture condenses, and a crest cloud forms as a standing feature. Now as the sky clears and the air cools, the wind cloud becomes a cottony, transparent mist. High cirrus clouds feather the skies in endless streaks, remnants of the day. The peaks on the west side of the John River are aglow with a pinkish color from the low-lying northern sun. Streaks of snow are brilliant, and the gray shales seem afire. The chill of the air hangs upon my eyelids and forces them to turn from the evening's beauty. Where my sleeping bag is damp from last night's rain a thin coat of flaky white ice has formed. I whisk the ice away and put my clothes into my stuff sack at the foot of my sleeping bag. Lying in my bag, I look at the feathered clouds as they change from white to pink to orange and lingering purple.

Arctic grayling

JULY 8

Morning comes delightfully to me this day. I have no watch or sundial, nothing to inform me where my modern counterparts in cities south of here are at this time, in their normal workday lives. It isolates me from any pressure of going so far every hour, or keeping to a schedule of meals or of quitting time. I keep a record of the date, and know that the "day of the week" will slowly drift away. My body and mind establish a rhythm for waking, walking, and taking meals—that is most natural and comfortable for me. I am finding it a perfect way to live, as I integrate facets of work and enjoyment throughout the waking day instead of limiting my enjoyment to after work or after walking periods.

I go along the river bars and sides as much as I can today. The rocks are not too large, and it is dry, although in many places, I must cross the river to gain access to river bars on the opposite side. Where the river meanders, water rushes along the outside of the bend, eroding the bank, and slack water is found on the inside of each bend.

In several areas on the outside of meanders where the river eats into the bank, the bank drops sheerly into the river, forcing me back into the verdure. The ground is wet and mossy with tussocks and hummocks. Hummocks are features built up in the same manner as tussocks—by the detritus of the plants that live on that spot. Tussocks, however, are made up of grass, cotton grass, and sedge, whereas hummocks are made up of moss, shrubs, and herbs. Hummocks are convex and several feet across and a foot or two high, measuring the difference from rim to center.

The north-facing slopes here are predominantly covered with heaths, blueberries, Labrador tea, and shrubby birches on the hummocks and tussocks. The Labrador tea is in flower, and its small clumps of white blossoms add color to the green of the leaf, and the brownish red stems of the birches. Mosses and lichens cover the grounds and are swollen with water. This adds a spongy, sinking-in nature to the already sloppy walking.

In sand along the river I come upon the tracks of a large canine with paws as big around as the palm of my hand; it must be a wolf. Its path leads up the Kollutarak and winds along the river. I follow the trail, as I know the animal has probably trotted up this valley many times and surely knows the most appropriate ways to travel. I notice that it too avoids the tussocks when possible, venturing onto river bars or across the river instead of into the vegetation. There is only one set of tracks, and I judge by the sharp outlines in the sand that this wolf has been here since the rains of yesterday. I wonder where it was headed. A meat eater like that must often get hungry in this country, but the animal's great potential for travel could soon put it somewhere that fulfills its need quite rapidly.

Several people told me before I came here that all I would need to survive in the way of food was fatty meat and a vitamin C source. Travelers have always had the problem of securing the latter. In alpine and arctic regions, an abundant plant called mountain sorrel (*Oxyria digyna*) is a good source of vitamin C and the most enjoyable edible native leaf I have ever tasted. Its crisp green leaves have a tang, like a spot of vinegar. Every hiker should know it. I find it in rocky areas, depressions, and along the riverbank, where snow accumulated in winter. Whenever I come upon a patch of it, I pick a handful of leaves and munch on them. Willow leaves probably contain vitamin C, too, but they are bitter.

I come to a steep gully, and decide to sit in its shade and drink some of its water. It is a small ravine, maybe twenty feet deep, with large rocks in the bottom and a tiny flow of water. There are a few tall willows, but aside from them, the soil is bare and seems to be composed of easily erodible shales. As I relax, a large bird noiselessly bobs by. It is an upland plover feeding on insects at the water's side. I think that its long yellow legs are seemingly in the height of fashion, and I laugh at myself, slightly embarrassed. It walks down the stream and two more, probably its progeny, follow about ten yards behind.

The day is overcast, calm, and gray. The Kollutarak valley is long and winding, with green-covered gray peaks springing from both sides of the valley. They are connected by jagged broken ridges of rock. The upper parts of many ridges are cliffs, forming spectacular walls. The sedimentary nature of the stone lends striated images to these cliffs, which make them seem all the more barren, forbidding, and impressive. The ridges are broken every few miles by side valleys, which take on the character of these cliffs—narrow, steep, abruptly bending and vanishing behind a ridge. These side canyons seem remote and endless, though from my maps I know that they are short, end against some nearby peak, and lead nowhere but to that peak. Their mystery is further enhanced by the lid of clouds that turns these canyons into caves, as if daring me to enter, explore, and take in their grand visions.

Along the river among a stand of small willows, I come upon a willow ptarmigan. This bird is the arctic cousin of the grouse. It is brownish red on its breast and back, with white wings. The plumage is solid white in winter, blending in with the snow, and changes to brown for the summer season. I stop and quietly unsling my pack. I find my goatskin gloves, unlash my bow, and attach its strings to both nocks. From my quiver I pull an arrow with a blunt head and feathers that wind around the shaft. This arrangement of feathers slows the flight of the arrow after a short distance, which is most useful when shooting at flying birds because the arrow will not fly too far. I put an arrow in place on the string, gently pull it back a few times, spot the bird in a clearing among the clumps of willows, and stealthily approach it. It seems to be feeding on leaves and something on the ground and pays me little heed. Walking crouched over, I move closer and it gazes at me and takes a few steps in the opposite direction. I get to within about thirty feet, my heart starting to accelerate with excitement, and move into a position that gives me a clear shot at its plump body. It all seems quite easy, and already I am anticipating the change of menu from grayling. I stop, brace myself, fix my eyes on its neck, raise my bow, draw back my arrow, and without a moment's hesitation, let it fly. Choom! The arrow zips along the bottom of its stomach, and the startled bird takes to the air. I run for my arrow and take up the chase.

The ptarmigan flies about forty yards up onto the hillside. The vegetation may be tussocks and I may be worn out from the day's labors, but I sprint with bounding excitement, adroitly stepping on and between tussocks. I keep an eye on the spot where it landed but know that birds like this sometimes land and then flee on foot among the shrubs and dense vegetation, which can swallow a motionless bird and render it invisible. I reach the spot and find no bird. I run a circle around the area, increasing the circumference, hoping to see it again. Whoosh. It flushes at my feet, arches to the sky, opens its wings to the breeze, and is gone in an instant. I take three steps in reflexed chase, then fall to the earth. My face lies against a mound of cotton grass, and my eyes are closed. There is not a sound but that of my breathing and the standing up again of plants that were flattened by my last steps. My panting soon ends and I roll over onto my back. I watch the clouds, and my field of vision, from the ground to the northern mountains, gives me the feeling that the sky is alive and moving. I run my hands through the vegetation at my side. The cotton grass is stiff though flexible, the birch is brittle, the other herbs are smooth. The lichens and mosses are wet, hairy, silky, and spongy. I think of that bird. I laugh, and know that the ptarmigan realized what almost happened. I'm sure it breathed in relief.

I walk back to my pack, bow in hand, and marvel at the jumble of up and down underfoot. I constantly lurch, stumble, sink, and slip. No wonder. With my pack on, it's such a pain just to walk. For a minute, I wish I were like the wolf and didn't have to carry my provisions and securities on my back. But if I could subsist here, as the wolf does, with nothing but my body and innate skills, then I would have no reason to be conducting this experiment now, trying to see what it is like living without the entrapments of civilization.

I begin to look at the vegetation for edibles, as they have a less fleeting nature than birds. Bistorts (*Polygonum bistorta* and *P. viviparum*) grow among the hummocks in drier spots. The large bistort (*P. bistorta*) stands a foot high with a bright plume of pink blossoms, making it impossible to miss it on the tundra. I nibble on a few of the younger leaves and find them quite palatable. Most wild leaves have a bitter taste, but these do not. I get to my knees and dig up the entire plant to sample the rhizome. Rhizomes are portions of the root system that are used by the plant for storing carbohydrates. Thus they are thick and can be sweet. This one is as large in diameter as a pencil and an inch and a half long with many bends. It is crunchy and a tiny bit bitter, but I think the bitterness can be dissipated with boiling. The rhizome of the smaller bistort (*P. viviparum*) is not bitter at all and is rather nutty tasting.

Along the river gravel the most common herb is river beauty (*Epilobium latifolium*), a small fireweed with a myriad of huge rosy flowers. This plant paints red and green upon the innumerable dull-colored cobbles of the riverside. I pluck a few of the youngest leaves from a plant and taste them. They are quite edible, but the older leaves lower on the stem are too bitter for my taste buds.

As I tire from river crossing, tripping on rocks, and fishing mosquitoes from my eyes, I look for a place to camp. A raised patch of fine gravel alluvium appears to offer a flat possibility, and the chance of the river rising and washing me away seems more pleasant than sleeping among the tussocks. I gather some rocks and catch some grayling, then, as my dinner starts cooking, I collect a handful of bistort roots and leaves and some fireweed leaves. I add them, along with the scaled, headless grayling, to the nearly cooked rice, barley, and split peas. It makes a diversified dinner. The roots keep their crunchiness and take on a milder flavor than when raw, which makes them a welcome addition. The leaves form floating masses of slippery vegetable. The bistort leaves are fine; the fireweed leaves are still bitter when cooked but do not spoil the pot.

As the clouds seem to be lowering, intent on touching the valley with their rains, I set up my shelter. I add two more poles, crossed and tied at the top, to give some elevation to the foot of the tent and alleviate the problem of a wet sleeping bag.

The ground is firm and flat. I watch the mosquitoes play against the orange material of the inside of my shelter. They don't bother me, though they congregate in vast numbers. Raindrops ring out on my roof, and where one hits the poncho, it jars the mosquitoes loose from that spot. They are sluggish and uninterested in me. I wish I had someone to talk to now. I realize the freedom that being alone brings, but now all I feel is the rain, the breeze, the rocks at my back. I am alone.

Willow ptarmigan

I crawl from deep piles of warmth to greet the day. At the stream I rub a handful of water, the water of millions of newly melted snowflakes, deep into my face and direct my skin to the breeze that tumbles down the valley. When I open my eyes, I gaze longingly at the valley that makes my day and my night, the valley that feeds me and warms me. How important it is to be friends.

I take slow pleasure this morning eating my granola breakfast and looking up the small valley that pours its water into the Kollutarak just across from where I am camped. The valley bends to the right along a dramatic wall and continues out of sight. The wall is high and broken and in one portion, rises to a sharp peak, curved and toothlike. Under its curve, the peak carries a huge bank of snow, and the whole wall itself is about half covered with white. Ledges on the wall, formed by more resistant sedimentary layers, also hold snow. Small gullies still hold drifts of snow that drip away to feed the creek. The hills that lie before the high wall are spotted with dark green shrubs at their highest elevations, and bright, light green herbs and shrubs on the low portions, where the wall merges with the valley bottom. The small tributary running through the valley forms a fanlike delta where it meets the Kollutarak. Felt-leaved willow, which has a bluer tinge than the other shrubs, conforms to the fan-shaped pattern. It prefers the coarse alluvium to the hillside soil, where the ground thaws to a greater depth than other areas. The stream flows to one side of the delta, not upon it. The scene holds my gaze because of its distinctive patterns and variety—from fan to hill to stream to stark peak and snow.

I am finding it easier each day to break camp. I develop a method for each thing, and know its place in my pack by second nature. Donning my pack, I find that it is becoming a fixed article of wear. I have not had a sore muscle or bruise so far, and I find the thought of having carried this pack in tussock country without any lingering physical ills to be quite reinforcing. The mosquitoes, too, are becoming just another part of the environment, and trouble me only when my pants are rolled up or pulled down.

I walk along the stream when I can, but find it impossible in many places because of dense shrubs, swift water, and dropoffs. I am starting to gain elevation rapidly and the valley is getting narrower. The north-facing slopes are still predominantly heaths, with net-leaved willows. Tall willows are now found only along the creek and tributaries. The blueberries have no flowers, and will have no berries this year. They must flower and fruit occasionally, even though their primary means of reproduction is stems rising from spreading roots.

Along the stream margins, the sounds of rushing waters, brushing shrubs, and plodding feet are occasionally interrupted by a most persistent streamside bird. The spotted sandpiper is very common along this stream, and is always roused for a high-pitched series of cheeps. It is a very small bird, about six inches long, with a white- and black-spotted breast. What it lacks in size, it makes up for in determination. One bird follows me up the creek with its "cheep, cheep, cheep." It just doesn't leave me alone as it parallels my progress on the other shore. A really persistent one takes over and follows me for about forty yards, then there is quiet again. But in another few hundred yards, there is another one. It is as if they have a communication system, to tell a friend upriver of my approach. They all know how to handle the situation, as each bird's treatment is identical to the bird's before. I feel picked upon and begin throwing rocks into the river, hoping that this will shoo them away, but it doesn't work, and I reluctantly take to the hillside and tussocks when I see one.

The day is turning warm and the sky a deep blue. I walk in the tussocks and hummocks for a mile and curse at them in seven languages—six of these invented at the time. Now to make progress, I must push myself. I scan the landscape for something that looks like relief and easier walking. I tell myself that it will be nicer ahead, even though I know that it will not be so.

Along the river's edge, I come to a spot that causes me to stop. The stream comes from a slightly higher level and makes a bend toward me. It cascades down a whitening riffle, broadening out into a most spectacular pool. Beyond the pool rises a huge, domed mountain. It has small buttresses at its summit and hills upon its flanks. These hills give it a gentle rolling look that scatters the pattern of vegetation into a mosaic of multi-shaded green. Patches of bare soils and rocks in steep areas further accentuate the striking sunlit-green appearance of the mountain. The alp impinges its grand silhouette upon the crystal blue of sky. The stream is braided here and enters the pool in four different segments, each addition of water further calming, deepening and organizing a body of still fluid. The color of the water is the color of the sky, and cobbles smoothed and rounded by many years' proximity to flow, comprise the streamside.

I drop my pack and piece together my fly rod. The pool is about fifty by twenty feet, and I speculate upon its bounty of grayling. I whisk my black gnat through the air several times and let it light upon the calm water. First working the back stretches of the pool, then the sides, and last the head, I pull six grayling from the water for sport, returning all unharmed. Maybe it's just the moment and the way the sun sits over my shoulder and the way I look at the delicate fish, but I see lavish color and detail that I have never imagined. Holding a fat fourteen-inch specimen in my wet hands along the water's surface, I see that its sides are a radiant translucent blue, and the head and tail are a solid green, blending toward the aquamarine of seawater. The pectoral fins are rainbows of stratified brilliance in green, brown, and white. The dorsal fin is a huge swaying appendage stretching from just behind the head to perhaps halfway to its tail. It is bespeckled with red, black, brown, and white dots, circles, and circled spots on a background of green. The body is also a pattern of scales, further set off by their overlapping and shading.

I walk a bit farther and find a nice, well-drained patch of vegetation along the stream bank. I break out my cornmeal-wheat biscuits and spread them liberally with honey, which I pour from a wide-mouthed plastic container. Lunch is always a sweet treat, and I try to make it last as long as possible. It is warm in the sun, and breezeless. I lie back on the luxuriant turf and stretch my body in every conceivable direction. Herbs brush my skin, and I dig my nose into the earth to smell its life. I feel strong and healthy.

One more roll and I sit up to see my honey jug lying overturned, with golden liquid reluctantly flowing on the sun-lit tundra. I leap to the spot and with the mouth of the bottle, scrape up all that I can. Honey is encrusted and entwined with reindeer lichens and mosses, and I add these seemingly petrified forms to my container. Some of the more sparingly coated pieces I let soak in my mouth, until all I can taste are the lichens, some of which are bitter, some tasteless. When it is all over but the crying, I see I have not lost that much, maybe a fifth.

Here I start to see a new plant, Alaska *Boykinia*, which is the tallest herb I have seen in the Brooks Range. It is a showy and beautiful species, endemic to northern Alaska. Up to two feet tall, it has clusters of five-petaled, starlike white flowers. Its basal leaves are broad, rounded, shiny, and spread abundantly above the ground. These plants stand as showpieces along the river, displaying how native species can survive the region's brutal winters and thrive in the brief summers.

Along the river, where the walking now is fine, I find stands of another plant I am just learning to recognize, Eskimo potato (*Hedysarum alpinum*). It grows in the gravel and well-drained areas, and I know it is eaten by natives. Bears gather it by tearing up huge mats of vegetation to find its thickened rhizomes. As there is another species (*H. mackenzii*) of the same genus that is reported to be poisonous, it is important for hikers to be aware of the difference between them: the safe Eskimo potato has conspicuous lateral veins on the leaflets; these veins are not visible in the inedible species. I do not carry any botanical text, but have these notes jotted down in my journal. After looking over several hundred plants and finding none of the poisonous species, I decide to try some. The ground is rocky and tough to dig in. I have no suitable tool to help me, so I just claw at the ground. There are many rhizomes that spread from the base of the roots, which are several inches deep. Some are swollen with starches, while others are thin and not used for storage. It takes a lot of work to loosen a series of these rhizomes and bring them to the surface. I wash the dirt from them in the creek, and try them, finding that they are far sweeter than anything I have tried thus far.

The wind picks up later in the day, and the chill quickly takes my sweat away. I don a coat and continue up a hillside, noticing that the ground here is better drained, and the tussocks only patchy and easily avoided. Here I discover yet another edible plant, a yellow-flowered vetch (*Astragalus umbellatus*). It is in full bloom, and its distinctive arrangement and light yellow color make it easy to recognize. There are huge stands of it here, and I find its root also quite fine eating, though stringy.

I believe that someone who was lost or hurt in these mountains, and who had run short or was out of provisions, could survive quite well on the wild plant foods of the area. Of course, to the unknowledgeable observer, it is just a bunch of weeds or grass, and the only edible things are caribou or fish. A little understanding of the food web of any area must start with the knowledge that all food energy comes originally from the sun. This energy is captured by green plants, which convert the radiant energy into sugars. Green plants are primary producers, and all other forms of life feed upon them, directly or indirectly. The amount of plant mass far outweighs the amount of animal material in almost any area. This is especially true in arctic situations where animals roam over many miles each year and, at certain times, some regions have few animals. The plants then are the most consistent and reliable form of wild food. Roots and sorrel, along with grayling or other fish, provide a well-balanced and pleasing diet.

Walking in the upper reaches of this valley is becoming nicer all the time. Slopes are drier, tussocks more scarce, and the valley is narrowing into a cozy home. I am starting to see that though my progress is slow, it is consistent, and I am reaching the head of this valley. Upon a raised bench on the south-facing slope I find a well-drained meadow. It reminds me of an alpine meadow in the Rockies, and is the first of its kind I have seen here. There are clumps of willows, up to a foot in height, mats of mountain avens, and a dwarf willow spread along the ground. The yellow vetch is in full bloom, along with bistort, moss campion, mouse-ear chickweed, a purple vetch, and a purple lousewort. Clumps and tufts and mats of flowering plants cover the entire meadow, and hardly a spot of bare soil shows through. Bunches of arctic poppies are still in bloom; their golden petals are starting to wrinkle with age, and they will soon fall.

The meadow is about two hundred yards long, and gives way in its upper stretches to wetter ground with the ubiquitous tussocks. I head for the stream, and the rocky shores and bars. Along the bank is a spot where a small gully merges with the stream, and tall willows fill the gully. I find a small village of arctic ground squirrels living there and am drawn to them by their warning cries. On a little rise downwind, I train my binoculars on the area. The high-pitched screeching goes on for some time, but they cannot smell or hear me and their eyesight is poor, so they soon go on with normal activities. The area is not rocky, and they don't stray far from the willows. They are about ten inches long, a little larger than other ground squirrels that I have seen in other regions of North America. They sit up next to their burrows and turn from side to side testing the air. After several minutes, I feel that they still can somehow sense my presence, and I strike off upstream. Native Alaskans call these quite abundant critters parka squirrels, and trap or shoot large numbers of them to make coats. The hides are very light in weight, but they are not so plush as mink or other furs and so are not in such great demand.

Small, dry hills are common now on the valley side, covered with mountain avens, heather, herbs, and grasses. A pair of American golden plovers seems to inhabit every hill. They are big land birds, eight to ten inches in height, and run across the tundra with such quickness that they rarely need to fly. Their neck, breast, and face are black, and the sides of their head and breast are white. The top of their heads and backs are a beautiful mottled gold. The migratory behaviors of these birds are amazing. Winters are spent in southern South America, and summers are spent nesting here in the North American Arctic—a trip of more than seven thousand miles each way. The birds here do not seem tired at all, but they do hesitate to fly. I know they must have nests around, and I search many hills and hill margins where I have seen the adults, but I find none. Each time the birds try to get me to follow them— "oodle, oddle," as they scamper quickly—I search in the opposite direction. I enjoy them and knowing that they fly so far just to spend the summer on these hills makes it seem like an even more special section of earth.

Ever since I made the first bend into the Kollutarak valley, I have looked up toward the end of the valley to see a pyramid-shaped mountain. Whenever walking has gotten tough, I have focused on that distant spot and said to myself, "I'll be there soon." It may take several days to reach a distant spot, as it did to reach this one, but when I think back to when I first saw the mountain, it gives me perspective on the large amounts of terrain I am covering. I feel it is my first milestone, though actually it is only twenty-five miles from the landing strip at Anaktuvuk Pass.

I pick up my pack and start on around the mountain. It rises right from the dwindling creek, rocky, loose, and shaly at its steep base, becoming gradually more vegetated upon its flanks and low summit. The creek waters are rushing and tumbling and pools are diminishing in size. I walk in tall willows on the flood plain and it is dry, but I thread my way among clumps of the waist-to-chest-high bushes. There are paths winding through the area, and I pick up a wad of material from a branch at pathside that puzzles me. It is composed of strands, but they are not woven, or so combed or so orderly as fur. It is pure white, and for a second I think it is the cotton from the willow catkins. But I see many catkins, and they are completely different. The material is oily and smooth, and small woolly fibers hold the mass together. Woolly! My eyes look up, excited, and there, as I guessed, standing by the creek looking back at me, are five Dall sheep. My heart is pounding, all pains and toils forgotten. This is why I had to come here. I look at the wild creatures as they ramble up a ledge fifty feet in front of me, and my mind is clear. These sheep are wild, the birds and plants and rivers are wild; I came here to feel wild, to be wild!

There are three ewes and two lambs; the adult males and females keep separate at this time of year. The sheep are pure white, lanky, and very picturesque as they amble slowly up the pyramid mountain, stopping to munch on plants. The lambs feed when the adults feed, and when they think they will be left behind, scramble to catch up. Just reaching the mountain is reward enough for me, but being greeted here by sheep makes the moment very special.

The wind is picking up now and dark clouds appear, spreading across the skies. Lapland longspurs sing to me from the willows, and I make my walking and plodding steps an accompaniment. I hear a flock of birds coming up behind me — "chee-chee-chee, chee-chee-chee" — on a burst of wingbeats, then they glide, flying into the wind, and I crouch down into the willows. They land all around me, and their red crown and black chin identify them as redpolls. Some of the birds have a white rump, some brown; the flock is probably composed of hoary and common redpolls flying together.

Beyond the mountain the valley opens up again, and a broad bowl stretches off to the north. It rolls up to and blends into the alluvial fans that pour from the high mountains there.

Up ahead a mile or so, I can see the pass that leads toward Chandler Lake. But it's been a long day, I've seen many miles, and the ground here is dry and homey. I find a lush meadow, and though the ground is not flat, I feel that the site is suitable; my standards for sites have changed. The soils are pebbly, and bistorts form a beautiful pink strata that stretches as far as I can see toward the northern snow-streaked peaks. There are also yellow flowers, prostrate willows, and some showy chrysanthemums. The whole layer of vegetation is colorful and condensed.

I start to set up my shelter and am visited by a long-tailed jaeger. It lands about forty feet away, and begins a long, vociferous spiel. Either I have interrupted something it was doing or my presence is not appreciated. I did not see where it came from and there is only one in sight. I finish my task and go about my chore of collecting dinner. I go to the stream to search for fish, but the meager amount of water does not hold much potential. I try a stretch of about a hundred yards and see none. I then try a tiny, rocky tributary that flows in from the northern bowl. Small willows up to one foot high drape over the side of the stream, and I tease my dry fly along these margins. I see one small grayling, but it is not very eager to dine on my presentation. I throw down my rod and go after him with my hands. Moving up the stream, being careful not to splash or kick rocks loose, I slowly slip my hand under the willow where he hides, and feel his body. I know that I must have my hand in position before grabbing, as any sudden motion will cause him to flee. I move along the underside of his body, but just as I prepare to grab, he is gone.

I go back to camp fishless and put away my rod. The jaeger is still here, and I get suspicious. I remember a story told by a friend who, on an ascent of Mount McKinley, had his packs raided by ravens. I enjoy the company of the bird, but make sure to keep my pack closed. The vegetation here is composed of many species that I use as a food source, and since I have secured no fish today, I dig lots of roots. The soil is very pebbly, and I have to dig down three or four inches to the rootstocks. Small roots of herbs and grasses and the thin, wirelike roots of sedges make the job difficult. My fingers work at the rocks and between the meshing roots and down along the rootstocks of bistorts, vetches, Eskimo potatoes, and fireweeds. My fingers have a tough time in the dirt, and I cannot dig too quickly. I try the handle of a spoon to help me pry rocks, but the spoon lacks my fingers' deftness and dexterity so I use it to dig only at what must be removed to get at the individual roots I seek. A shovel would be a luxury. I spend an hour or so rummaging among the offerings of the earth and come up with enough to assist my rice in satisfying my appetite.

I put them in my pot and go down to the stream to wash them and carry water back. On the way I find several old Dall sheep skulls. There are no bodies, and one skull has an enormous, full-curl set of horns. These sheep were obviously killed by people seeking meat, not trophies, and I suspect the Nunamaiut were probably delighted to carry these carcasses home many years ago. The John River valley near the village is littered with skulls of caribou, probably left in the spot of the animals' death as the bodies were taken for food. Many of the skulls still support the massive, branched antlers of adult males, covered with lichens. These sheep skulls, and the memory of the caribou skulls, remind me that the primary foods of these native people are big game animals. I wonder if, in times of need, they too took to the soil for the foods they needed.

The limitless supplies of big game animals in this region are gone. The Nunamaiut must travel many miles to find caribou. Sure, I occasionally see animals, but I am crossing many, many miles. This land does not support the great number of resident animals that one would expect in undisturbed country, because the growing season is too short and the winters too severe. Caribou are migratory, using the country only in the spring and fall as they migrate to calving grounds north of the Brooks Range, then back to wintering grounds to the south. The number of animals is dwindling, perhaps because of increasing human hunting pressures. Visitors should not expect to live off the land by hunting big game. Small game, vegetable foods, and fish are plentiful, however, and can be used as a consistent supplement to whatever supplies are brought in. Early explorers depended upon big game to feed themselves, as anyone who has read the accounts of one of America's most influential conservationists, Bob Marshall, knows, though the carcasses were used only partially and could not be carried, as the explorers moved on. That cannot be done today, both because the game populations are now reduced and because this practice would further reduce the populations as the number of visitors increased.

I am having a problem finding wood now. The willows at streamside are quite small, and the largest dead twig I can find is about one foot in length and a quarter inch in diameter. I collect handfuls of these and start to wonder whether I will be able to find any wood at all on the other side of the pass, which separates Pacific and Arctic draining streams. The Kollutarak drains into the Pacific. The other side is Arctic draining water, and I fear that whatever slightly more arctic effects there may be could reduce the wood supply from this meager amount. To cook my food each night, I have to keep a fire burning for about forty minutes, and even making a fire that is two or three inches across, and adding one two-inch piece of twig at a time, still takes some wood. A camp stove would be nice in situations like this, but I could never have carried enough white gas to merit the luxury of it; the extra weight would have been unbearable. The wood gathering takes time, too — about twenty minutes for me to gather enough wood just for this fire. All the minutes spent in gathering wood, other fuel, and food, and preparing one meal take up a large portion of each day.

This night is typical of my inability to sleep soundly on this trip. The ground, a profusion of lumps and bumps, slopes toward the stream. A survey of all the possibilities of comfort and discomfort is made in the first half hour of lying on it. I choose the most adequate and least crippling position to start. Any noise keeps me awake, or wakens me from one of these uncomfortable positions and marginal states of sleep. The wind comes up the valley and shakes my shelter. The rain falls and enlivens the inside of my abode with the magnified echoing pats and splats of drops. I think, "Is my pack tightly closed?" though I know it is. "Is that jaeger out there looking for a meal?" and I hear steps, pulling, and pecking, though there are no such noises. "Have the hot rocks left over from my fire burned down into the humus and set the landscape afire?" But I know that, like every other night, I put the rocks into the stream so that the water could wash away the charcoal of fire and with it any evidence of my presence here. The rainwater pools up in the low spots along the margins of my shelter and I think the water is getting deeper and will pull down my sleeping quarters. I kick and push at the sides to drain the water, though it doesn't need it.

"Night" goes on like this, with bits of sleep scattered throughout. There must have been long periods of sleep, though, for when it is time to push some of the water from my shelter, a multitude of mosquitoes circle my face. I keep the bottle of mosquito repellent near my head in my shelter and put on a few drops to aid me in attaining a few more minutes of sleep. I am lazy this morning. It has rained and the vegetation is wet. I have no great ambition to rush out into the soggy terrain, and know that if I wait just a few more minutes, it will dry.

I pack up and eat my granola. The clouds still hang near, draped upon the mountains, graying the sky. I start off toward the pass that will take me to Chandler Lake. The valley turns into a tussock paradise. From mountain to mountain the only vegetation is tussocks, which are knee-high, with four inches of water running among them. There's no way out of them or around them. I hate to sit down because everything is wet. The mosquitoes cover me, get in my eyes and ears, and catch in my throat on a deep breath. I hate the country. I don't know why I'm here when I could be hiking in a less demanding part of the world.

I head for a slope to the south and climb up to what the map shows to be a broad open area, hoping the increase in elevation will provide the extra drainage that will eliminate the tussocks and bring back my appreciation of the country. But I find myself in miles of bigger tussocks. I climb up on a ridge that separates the valley from this basin. It is made up of boulders of every size and shape. Patches of mountain avens and other turf-forming species are mingled occasionally with the smaller rocks. I play like a daring leaper, spanning distances between huddled rocks, knowing that I must balance myself perfectly before each leap or my pack will throw me off kilter and I will fall and break my body in every conceivable place. Then I will have to lie here until the snows come and bury me under a frozen blanket. Yet I would rather take a chance on breaking my neck on these boulders than spend five more minutes with those tussocks.

I come to the end of the ridge, and about a thousand feet below me opens the valley that leads to Chandler Lake, which I can see in the distance. The valley, a broad sweeping U lined with green, is gracefully awesome. The walls are steep and frame the portion of the lake now visible in a marvelous picture. The lake looks white, and my binoculars reveal that it is still mostly frozen. The little unnamed stream that drains the valley winds, capricious and uncaring, wherever it may through the broad valley bottom.

I descend the ridge and follow a small stream that drains from the south, from the snowfields of Mount MacVicar (MacVicar was a botanist who visited this area in the early

1900s). It has willows along it, and I am relieved. Though it does not have a broad flood plain like the Kollutarak, it does have some rocky, dry country. The stream is swift, and many small boulders fill the channel. I want to cross the stream, but the water is deeply pooled or moves swiftly over slippery rocks that do not seem very appealing. A half mile downstream, a crossing appears nice enough to try with my boots on. Changing into sneakers then back to boots is a time-consuming chore; and whenever a crossing is feasible in boots, I go ahead. To make this crossing, I step from the bank out onto a large boulder, and then skip in three jumps toward the other bank. I slip off one rock and find myself knee-deep, and end up taking off that boot anyway when I reach the opposite bank in order to change socks.

A talus slope comes down almost to riverside, and the shrill whistling of a hoary marmot fills the air. It takes a while for me to spot one, because their grayish bodies blend in with the light-colored rocks and the drab tone of the day. I see one nearby in the rocks and I am surprised at its great size. It is over eighteen inches long and would weigh more than fifteen pounds. I think of my stomach, then of my ability as an archer, and I move on.

I walk toward the center of a beautiful arctic valley. Two long-tailed jaegers fly by and land fifty feet in front of me. I stop to listen to their discourse and get a good look at their distinctive plumage. What well-adorned creatures they are, with a black head crown, white neck and belly, a bit of yellow on the back of the neck, and light gray on the back and wings. Two of the tail feathers extend beyond the normal length of tail for most birds and are much longer than those of other species of jaegers. They must form a rudder for this bird's effortless gliding flight. In general shape and behavior, these jaegers remind me of the magpie. Sitting on some tussocks, I happen to notice a movement in the vegetation. It turns out to be a ptarmigan and five babies. I have to focus and refocus even to see the little ones, they blend in so well. The adult is brownish and smaller than the first ptarmigan I chased. This bird, however, is more important raising its young than it ever could be in my pot. It could be a rock ptarmigan, as it is smaller, but I do not guess at identification.

I follow the stream where possible, staying on its sandy bars and banks. I find myself having to take running broad jumps with a full pack to try to reach a sandbar on the opposite side of the stream. I land with a splash and the water comes up over my boots and inundates my pants. I head for the junction of the southern valley wall and the valley bottom, hoping to find more rocky soils and drier ground. But it is not so. Tussocks, small and steep gullies, rock piles, and what are known as solifluction terraces—lobes of soil that move downhill —make up the jumbled terrain. But I can see Chandler Lake, and I am excited.

White spots are high on the mountainside to the north, and I want to identify them as sheep, but I can't. Many times when resting, I study my maps. I like to study each new valley, learn every peak, and identify every new ridge, hill, and valley. That way I feel familiar with the country. My maps are rolled up in a red plastic fishing rod case. It has pieces that fit over each end, and it is quite waterproof. Now I reach for it and do not find it. I panic, frantically taking everything out of my red pack, scraping the sides to see if the case has just been camouflaged and I can't see it. Thinking back to where I last looked at maps, I remember using them early this morning on the rock ridge that overlooks this valley. I look up the valley to where the rocky ridge is and feel ill. It must be four or five miles. Talking myself into believing that I dropped the case somewhere as I rested, I prop my pack up on a small hill so I'll be able to see it upon my return and set off with my binoculars up the valley. I try to follow the same route back, but looking at things in the reverse direction now is like looking at them for the first time. I can guide myself along some of the larger slides, rock piles, and the ponds, trying to remember all the places where I had stopped to look at the flowers, all the places where I had rested, the spots along the pond margins where I had looked deep into the fluid to see if anything was living in those waters. My pace is wild, damned near running. My feet feel light, the buoyancy being a product of my desperation. I must find those maps. I probably can find my way to the Alatna River from here without them, as I had studied the maps for many hours, but maps are more than that for me. There are countless things to learn from them, and besides, looking at them each evening and seeing my progress is inspirational. It gives me the motivation to rise the next morning and do it again.

I walk and walk, climbing each hill and rock pile to get a view of the terrain and scanning every inch with my binoculars. I must have walked two or three miles when I cross a small gully, and coming up the other bank, my heart quickens. There is my red case. One of the end pieces is off, and I think that my maps have maybe fallen out, but I realize happily that they are inside. I scream and yell in victory, though I have done nothing superb, just made up for a stupid error. If my case had not been red, I would have had no chance of finding it. I run all the way back to my pack, not exactly having an easy time finding it either.

I hurry on to Chandler Lake, worn from my extra five or so miles of movement. Just where the valley opens, almost at lakeside, are terraces, with mountain avens, an anemone, heather, and bistorts together and all in flower. One lobe higher up the hillside is large enough and dry enough to provide space for the evening. The sky is breaking now and patches of blue are showing through. I piece together my fishing pole and go to the lake. I remember now the natives had told me, with outstretched arms, how big the lake trout can get. The lake is about five miles long and one mile wide. Its long axis trends northeast, southwest, in a snug valley where steep mountains rise from both sides. The center of the lake is still sealed in ice. On this eastern side, the ice is about a hundred feet from shore. The shoreline is rocky, and the water is quite shallow as far out as I can see. A few clumps of willows line the shore, just high enough to catch my dry fly as I cast. What a mess it makes of my line. I can see no fish—no grayling, no trout. I walk up the shore and am attacked by an arctic tern. The first time it swoops by, I don't understand and am delighted by its visit. Its red bill and black crown flash in the brightening sun, and it wheels around and comes back. It flies as a weightless object, almost like a boomerang but bobbing from side to side, with long, pointed wings stabbing at the air. Its forked tail and dangling reddish legs become obvious as it nonchalantly comes close and then suddenly dives at me, missing my head by about two feet. I see that this fellow means business. It must have a mate and a nest nearby. I let the tern shoo me away and turn to go fish in the stream.

Where the stream merges with the lake, it slows, loses its ability to carry what sediment it does move, and there builds a silty, sandy deposit. This deposit is waterlogged like quicksand and will not hold my weight, which I find out by stepping onto it and going in knee-deep. I follow the stream up into the valley. It meanders smoothly, creating broad deep pools, and has steep banks with patches of willows. It looks perfect for fishing, but I see no grayling in the crystal water, feel no tugs at my fly. I go back to camp, fishless again, and wish I had a spinning rod to cast some shiny lures out to the edge of the ice and entice some lunker lake trout.

Bistorts are common, as is fireweed, so I cook up a vegetable soup and add two heaping spoons of lard to enrich my meal. Wood here is more scarce than it was last night. I really have to scrounge among the willows for a small bundle to fire my meal. Walking here is poor, even without a pack, because of the tussocks, so I stick to my campsite for the remainder of the evening and explore the area visually. Across the lake, mountains rise several thousand feet, forming a spectacular ridge. The ridge is dissected by small drainages, giving the impression that many mountains have been squashed and shoved together. Patches of snow linger on some of the mountains, and the circumference of each rocky peak is outlined clearly by the bluing sky.

In many mountain ranges, the greatest beauty lies in its peaks, alone or clustered. Looking at the Brooks Range, I feel its beauty is in the valleys—wide, graceful, arching plains, with steep symmetrical side walls, and magnificent alluvial fans that spread from every interlude in the valley walls. The most lingering image is the greenness. In the sunshine against the blue sky, nothing is more green than this dwarf, undulating growth.

Everything is on such a grandiose scale here—the mountains, the lake, the valley. I feel dwarfed. I can see a nearby peak pointing to me, and I seem to hear a deep echoing voice. Then it is quiet and the sun moves behind the mountains to the northwest. The sky clears and I know it will be a cool evening.

The ridge across the lake runs to the north, withers, and ends, giving way to a few small, round hills. Beyond that the landscape flattens into what I know is the North Slope, the great Arctic plain beyond the Brooks Range. The blue sky fades to gray blue, and the sun rolls out from behind the ridge and hills. The valley of the Chandler is open to the north, and there at the horizon sits the sun. The valley seems like a long tunnel, lined with bodies of water, golden sides, verdant flanks, and sharp ridges, with the glowing orange ball at its far end. I lie in my sleeping bag as a fine layer of frost forms on the soil and damp foliage. The ice on the surface of the lake is alive with the imparted colors of the sun. I rest, calling the day to a close. The sun is gaining altitude toward the northeast. A new day has already begun.

The waters of Chandler Lake are still and mirrorlike, reflecting the mountains, hills, and puffs of clouds. The sun is warm, and a floating mass of ice, separate from the main sheet, drips water onto the calm surface, sending out pulses of rings, concentric, spreading, and fading. It is the only disturbance this morning of the enchanting environment.

I start walking south along the rocky shoreline. There are low, swampy areas and higher, rocky, drier areas. Of course, tussocks mingle among even the nicest. The nearshore portion of the lake seems to be very shallow and rocky. Vegetation covers a large part of the slope and is absent on only the vertical faces of the tallest rocks. I come upon a gathering of ten ptarmigan, all fully grown. I drop my pack and grab my bow. These birds are not willing to sit and watch me, and take off running as soon as my feet stop. I chase an individual as the group scatters in every direction. They find perfect cover and concealment among the rocks and shrubs. I see the top half of one bird about forty feet away and I set to shoot. I pull back and my arrow flies right on target, seemingly going through the bird, but the ptarmigan flies away. An examination of my arrow shows no blood, only feathers. The bird lands a hundred yards away, and I look around for another. I take four or five shots, all at good targets, and it's not that I miss by much, it's just that I miss enough each time that I walk from the situation with not one bird. It has actually been entertaining to chase the birds around, and it has given me a good warm-up for the day, but no meat. I have broken only one arrow during the barrage, but arrows cannot do me any good unless I can squarely hit the target. I can see I have little reason to carry them.

The head of Chandler Lake is sandy, and the valley turns into a large, poorly drained basin, dotted with ponds and ribboned with streams and tributaries. It presents a soggy situation about four or five miles long, continuing farther up the valley. I know there are even more miles of poorly drained country before reaching the next major body of water, Amiloyak Lake. At the head of Chandler Lake is the wreckage of a small plane, which probably had crashed while taking off or landing on the water or ice of the frozen lake in winter. This plane is not broken up too badly, but another plane sits mangled upon the hillside far above. Rescue in this country is slow for incidents like this, and these hulks make walking seem like a safe way to travel. The plane that I walk up to is completely stripped inside, and only the shell is left.

This basin is joined by a huge valley from the west, and the area takes on an open appearance, much like the open area where the Kollutarak River meets the John River. I come upon the carcass of a large Dall sheep that is many years old. It is intact except that the head is missing—obviously the produce of a trophy hunter who now hangs the head on his wall while the body sits here slowly rotting. It is wasteful and tragic that an animal like this should be killed just to boost someone's ego.

I find myself on the basin bottom in a sedge meadow, flat looking and consistent. What I could not see but now feel is that this whole bottomland is really a giant pool of water and the sedges merely grow in the shallower areas. The whole lower part of the basin probably was part of Chandler Lake many years ago. The debris brought in by the streams that settled here gradually filled in parts of the lake, allowing vegetation to take root. Tiny bits of dead plant matter from this vegetation, along with the accumulation of sediments, buried this part of the lake. The main part of Chandler is deep, scoured out by glaciers. The build-up of sediment has been going on mainly at tributary mouths and lake margins. The bottom portion of the basin is unwalkable, as the water is at least ankle-deep. The tussocks are dry and pleasant in comparison with these sedge areas.

Here and there, a small hill or ridge interrupts the uniformity of tussocks. Sometimes these hills are dry, and I walk hundreds of yards out of my way just to get onto one of them. The relief from having to raise my feet up to knee height is exquisite. It is grueling, nasty work carrying a hundred pounds plus myself through this endless expanse. I come to a small hill, spotted about a quarter mile away with my binoculars, and fall at its base exhausted. I lie still for several minutes and then sit up. I have had enough. I can't force myself to get up. I wish a helicopter would come and lift me out of here. I hate this ruthless basin and I don't want to be here. I try to stand up and take three steps, but I can't push myself any longer. I can't fool myself any longer. I just don't want to move anymore.

I scan the basin with my binoculars and pick out a route along ridges and the river. I stand and move away from the hill, as if casting a small boat from safe mooring in a harbor, out into a great churning sea. In this sea of tussocks, difficulty in walking comes in waves with crests and troughs. I feel as if I am fighting to make my way across some huge body of water and the waves are pushing me back. A crest of difficulty slows me, then passes, and I slide into the trough and gain some ground. I stop and eat dried apricots and drink a glass of richly prepared powdered milk. I wait until the food's energy spreads through my body and then push off again.

The day is hot, and I am soaked with perspiration. The mosquitoes are abundant and aggressive and my sweating makes frequent reapplication of repellent necessary. Occasionally, I wear my head net, but I would rather face the insects. My cotton hat is too heavy to wear anymore. I take out a handkerchief and make it into a turban that covers my head and comes down over the top portion of my sunglasses, shading my eyes. It is cooler, but I still sweat as if I am digging ditches in humid, hundred-degree weather. The mosquito repellent drips with my sweat and occasionally a drop of the mixture strikes my lip and numbs it for a few minutes. It is nice to know that the repellent is so strong, and I disregard the possible bodily side effects.

One hill I come upon is carpeted with mosses, blueberries,

lingonberries, and a whole assortment of grasses and shrubby willows. I look longingly at the vegetation and at this island it calls home. When I look to this earth, with all its browns and greens, I see life-forms striving to survive when to die would be so easy.

I walk toward the center of the basin and see a river terrace some distance off that looks dry and free of tussocks. The terrace runs parallel to, and is on the opposite side of, the stream. I come to a small moving body of water that connects two of the ponds. It is clear, about fifteen feet wide, and about ten feet deep. I would never try to cross it. I follow it upstream, but tussocks run to its banks and it provides me no potential for reaching the basin center. I strike off toward the valleyside again.

A major tributary comes in from the east now, and the country is lower and more dissected. There are gullies with ridges among them. In one place there is a most unusual stand of tall willows. They must be five feet tall, and though the stand isn't thick, it is carpeted with an orange sphagnum moss. It is another small colorful island, another bit of relief, maybe a hundred feet long, then back into the strips of tussocks I go. Gullies form the interlude to these strips. I come around the last pond of the wet portion of the valley, and I can see that the terrace on the opposite side of the stream is still running up the valley parallel to me. It is about one mile away, in the center of the basin, and I plan a route to follow a gully down, cross the stream at a wide spot, and get onto that terrace.

The gully is dry and sandy with many willows. I cross the tributary that comes in from the east, as it doesn't have much water in it. Then it's off across the tussocks to the main stream. It is broad, though not really swift, so I find an area of riffle, put on my sneakers, shoo away the droves of insects, roll up my pants, and splash into the water.

I run to the side of the terrace, which is adjacent to the stream, and stretch out. I take off my sneakers and let the water on my feet evaporate. The sides of the terrace are dry, composed of a gray siltlike deposit. Mountain avens and dwarf willows grow upon it, and not much else. I dry off and climb the thirty or so vertical feet to the top of the terrace. It is like being in a different world. The top is bone dry and flat. Bits of gray shale cover the ground in a range of sizes, giving me the feeling of being in a desert. I feel dry and hot, looking upon the flat surface. Thinking back to the vertical nature of tussocks, I feel happily disoriented. Vegetation here is scattered and very sparse. There are small patches of mountain avens and sandwort, and strawberry saxifrage is abundant. This saxifrage is most amazing and unusual. It is about four inches tall, with a small golden-yellow flower at its top. There is a tiny clump of leaves at the plant's base, and several long red stolons, which are trailing leafless stems, arch away from the base. Each stolon has a bud or bulbette at its end, which can root and reproduce the entire plant. This stolon or runner acts as an umbilical cord to the parent plant, and nourishment is provided until the bulbette can root and sustain itself. The common strawberry plant has similar reproductive methods.

Reindeer lichens are scattered along the ground in tufts and tangled masses, like a fairyland of dwarfs. The terrace soon ends, however. The paradise is short-lived, and tussocks and hummocks resume their supreme reign over the landscape.

I hike and hike in the same type of misery for what seems like an eternity. I want to make it to Amiloyak Lake today. I come upon a bend where the stream cuts at the bank, slows, and deepens into a lovely pool. I drop my pack to have a few minutes of fishing, and tell myself I will go on hiking after this brief rest, but I know I will stay here for the night. There is a flat area between several hummocks in one spot, and I lay out my bag there. I piece together my fishing pole and whip out my black gnat. The grayling here are great sport and rise to my fly just as if I had told them how to do it. I bring three fat fourteen-inchers onto shore and keep them. I catch another six or eight and release them unharmed. Then I start to look for wood. There isn't any! I find some six-inch-long twigs from shrubby birches on the hummocks and more of the same size stuff from streamside willows. I gather for perhaps a half hour and come up with a pretty meager bunch, including a handful of last year's dried flower stalks from herbs, mostly lousewort. It looks like a pile of wood, but I know each stick will burn only a few moments. I will have to budget the wood well or I will be eating raw fish and crunchy rice. The one thing I don't have to worry about is finding kindling because that's all there is. The mountains are made of shale, so there are no rocks upon which to prop my pot. I use my tent poles to build a tepee and dangle my pot from a string. I keep my fire tiny and the pot about two inches above it. I consider breaking up my tent poles and stakes to use as firewood, but I decide to do that only as a last resort.

Everything gets cooked, however, slowly but surely, and the warm fish soup soothes my pains away. The sun slips below the western mountains, and a chill immediately overcomes me. The refracting rays of the sun light up the mountains to the east, and their pink colors are reflected from the still water of the pool and from riffles. I leave everything as it is, not packing or putting anything away, and go find my sleeping bag. I know tomorrow will bring more of the same country I have plodded through today. But I feel it can't go on forever, and that satisfies me. Two mergansers flying hurriedly northward about ten feet above my head shatter the stillness of the air. Then it is quiet, and I lay my head net next to my bag in anticipation of the morning mosquito attack. A longspur is in the birch singing songs, and I find peace and comfort in this dry spot.

The mosquitoes are at me as the first rays of the sun fill the valley and warm their cold-blooded bodies into movement. I slip on my head net and smile, having outwitted them. I can now relax as the day warms up and my courage builds to get up and fight with tussocks.

I start up along the west-facing slopes toward Amiloyak Lake, climbing steadily, and I soon come to the lake, which is about one mile long and a few hundred yards wide. The center portion is still frozen, and the scene is almost barren of color. The day is building with clouds, and the tussocks here are tan, not green.

I come down a little closer to the lake for a look and am attacked by an arctic tern. It comes from a point that juts out into the lake, and I presume it has a nest there. It threatens me in the same manner as the last tern had done. I hike away from the lake to escape its wrath, but it is very persistent, following for hundreds of yards, swooping and screaming and very adequately driving me off.

I am approaching the Continental Divide and will soon be in Pacific draining valleys again. The passes here are very gradual, and the valley is narrower than down below. The top of the pass—flat and broad, with no definite boundary—seems as if it is just a few miles ahead. I can see over it and down the sides of the adjoining valley. There is a high mountain far down the valley that stands a bit above all others on that ridge. It is like the pyramid-shaped peak in the Kollutarak had been for me, and I look at it and talk to it constantly. I feel isolated now, much as that mountain must feel isolated, as it is set apart from all others. I think of civilized life many miles away and the easy life people live there. My days here are busy, and my mind is always occupied with the things I must provide for myself and the constant struggle to move and keep healthy. I wonder how these days are affecting my outlook on civilization.

Rain starts to pat down and the wind rustles the cotton grass. Dark clouds converge in the skies above and extend their shredded fingers toward me. I see a large erratic—a boulder left by a glacier—and spread my rain poncho from the top of the rock toward the ground. I put small rocks around to keep it in place and crawl under my makeshift shelter, propping up one end with my tent poles so I can see out. Rain comes down harder than it has at any other point on the trip. I put on my wool sweater and wool shirt, my down vest, and my parka, and I am still cold. The wind blows through my flimsy shelter, and I imagine it will fall down at any moment. I unroll my sleeping bag, take off my boots, and crawl in. I lie bathed in orange light filtered by my poncho and wonder what other people are doing now in lives where they do not have to stop what they are doing because of the weather. I would keep walking in this measly rain, but I know that to get wet and take a chance on getting everything wet, is the wrong thing to do. I must play by the land's rules and not try to fight it any more than I already have to with each step. If this land were to flex its muscles, I would surely be crushed.

After several hours of being cooped up, dozing, dreaming of other places, and writing, I stick out my head and see a patch of blue. I break camp and head for the pass. The drainage is very poor, as the ground that has tussocks is still saturated from spring, and no water can sink into the ground. I slosh toward the pass, slipping and splashing. Water comes over my boot tops and I can feel my toes swimming in my wet wool socks. I stop to change them, but realize that they will be wet again in a few moments. I start to think about my future and guess that I will have about one more week of walking in these broad valleys with low, flat bottoms. These valleys and their basement of permafrost are large accumulation basins for moisture and decaying organic material. This is represented in the tussocks, hummocks, and their wet character.

I look for a stopping point, as I imagine my feet to be suffering ill effects from their aqueous environment, and find a patch of mountain avens out in the middle of the streaming tussocks. It is an amazing island—dry, inhabited by bistorts and other edible species, with flowing water all around it, and just large enough to be homey for an evening. I pay so dearly for every moment's pleasure.

Luckily I find enough shrubby birches on the surrounding hummocks to kindle my fire, and since the evening skies seem to be clearing and tomorrow holds the promise for adequate supplies of willows, I burn my tent poles in order to cook dinner. It is a gray evening, still damp and humid from the afternoon's showers. Mosquitoes are everywhere, covering my sleeping bag and clothes. Cold comes gradually, catching the mosquitoes unsuspecting and unprepared—they seem to stiffen all at once. On my sleeping bag, hundreds of incapacitated insects stand or lie. I pick up the bag and shake them off like crumbs from a tablecloth. They sit paralyzed upon my knee and boot top, and I flick them off with my finger, relishing my revenge.

I dream that I am rescued from this drowning island, plucked from it and brought back to the civilization that I am accustomed to. It is a confusing experience, for as soon as I am let back into the land of houses, streets, and power poles, all I wish is to be back here—in the wilderness, on this island, my home for these hours. It reminds me of a Robert Service poem in which he says when you are in the north you cannot wait to get out, and when you are out you cannot wait to get back.

Morning comes refreshingly. I automatically slip on my head net as I hear the enlivened mosquitoes. I wonder whether some of these are the furious individuals I teased last evening. The sky is clear in every direction and I start off toward Agiak Lake. I am over the pass unknowingly and after a small decrease in elevation, see the lake. I hurry as quickly as possible through the tussocks and soon sit on the lakeshore. The ground is drying and Agiak is serene. Small willows circle the lake, and small hills flank its western shore. The hillsides are covered with hummocks that support a plant that is new to me—cloudberry (*Rubus chamaemorus*). It is in full bloom and hundreds of its white blossoms sparkle upon the rolling hummocks. The fruit of this plant is delicious and unique. Each plant supports one flower; some of the flowers are male, some female. The flowers, though, are susceptible to heavy frost, and probably produce fruit only in mild years, which this may be. I would like to be here when the cloudberries are ripe.

I walk along the hills and look down into the lake, which is oval and has an inlet on its eastern side and an outlet that flows southwest. It is shallow at the shore, but deepens more quickly than did Chandler Lake. I see grayling swimming lazily in the still water, slowly sweeping their tails back and forth, rising repeatedly to take insects. The water is calm, ice-less, soundless. Even the mosquitoes seem to quiet down for this moment of acute awareness. The ridge that runs away to the northeast toward Amiloyak Lake is dissected into tall, coaly sentries, lined up to watch the valley. Directly across the lake is another series of almost black mountains. A snow-covered group contrasts the black and is outlined against the clear, blue sky. It is all reflected from the lake waters in a stunning display, which gives symmetry to the hulking mountains. It is so naturally calming and enthralling that I do not want to leave this spot. But to the north, the sky is becoming smeared with delicate wisps of high cirrus clouds, and I still have a long way to go.

I start off toward the south, following the length of the lake. It is nice walking on the dry hilltops, and mats of brittle lichens crunch under my feet. I come down from a hill to Agiak Creek. It is swift and cold, but I cross it to reach another set of hills that runs along the opposite side of the creek. I can see many series of dry hills on down the valley and am thrilled about the possibilities of comfortable walking. It's such a nice relief from tussocks that I do not mind the constant up and down of the hills. And I do not mind crossing the stream innumerable times to walk on hills on the other side. I come upon a palsa now. A palsa is a feature, about the size of an automobile, formed when ice builds up on top of the permafrost. The ground surface rises like a blister and the vegetation rises with it, splitting at the top.

These hills are brown, and the growing season for them must have come and gone already. Lichens form a dominant cover in some areas, and the growing season is whenever unfrozen moisture becomes available. The streamside, though, is bright green with willows that now and then reach up to eight feet. Herbs are also abundant along the stream, and sand and gravel bars are pink with flowering fireweed. I try everything for taste—grasses, sedges, herbs, willow leaves, roots—anything to learn something.

Today I have the best day of walking that I have had so far, making ten to twelve miles. The rolling dry hills spoil me. Whenever I have to descend from a hill and search for another hill and end up walking a mile or two in the same old tussock-type vegetation that I have been walking in since the first hours of this trip, I am unnerved. I lose whatever calmness I have learned in days gone by for dealing with just such walking situations. I feel as if I have to get out of these tussocks or they will swallow me alive.

I find a nice flat area next to some rocks just above the stream, and decide to make camp. This place has everything I need. I make new tent poles from dead willow branches to re-place the poles I had burned last evening. I select only the straightest and srongest—those that will bend and flex in the wind without breaking. I remove all the peeling bark, expos-ing the smooth, brown gray tones of weathered wood. On rainy mornings I may be looking at these poles for many hours and want them to be visually pleasing. I collect longer poles than the last batch to provide more headroom for writing, reading, and just rolling over without rubbing the top of my shelter. This will also accommodate more mosquitoes! The area abounds with green herbs in their prime. I collect a potful of fireweed, bistorts, and rhizomes, and sample a new herb, sweet coltsfoot (*Petasites frigidus*), which has an edible root and fairly palatable leaves. There are also great clumps of sorrel around the rocks, and I make a salad of their greens, mixing in some willow and bistort leaves.

The stream provides me with everything that I could ever ask for in the way of fish. There are as many twelve-inch gray-ling as I want. I take four, then catch another dozen just for fun and release them unharmed. I make a luxurious fire from the abundant dead willow branches and have the best meal of the trip thus far.

Clouds make a darkening appearance at the end of dinner and let out some of their aggression on this valley. I crawl into my newly heightened abode, which feels like a real palace now. I lie as this Brooks Range thunderstorm pours out rain, thunder, and lightning. The thunder rolls up the valley in great rumbling pulses. Rain comes with a flash of lightning cracking on a nearby mountaintop. The ground becomes wet and swollen and takes on the refreshing flow of moist vege-tation.

The area is well drained, west facing, with moderate slope. Lingonberry (*Vaccinium vitis-idaea*) is the dominant plant. It is a dwarf evergreen shrub, which can produce deliciously tart berries. These berries usually ripen late in the summer, freeze on the plant, and can be picked in the spring. Unfortunately there are none now. Some of its leaves are red, some half red and half green, some yellow, and some green. The leaves are about a half inch long, oval, and shiny. The lingonberry plant is mixed with the miniature coniferlike Labrador tea, which has clusters of white and pinkish flowers at the ends of branches. Its leaves are dark green with the edges rolled under. Every inch of ground surface here is covered with an array of light green and brown reindeer and Iceland lichens. The whole composition of various dwarf forms and brilliant colors makes this three-inch-high layer of vegetation the most amazing entity anyone could ever hope to see.

Mountain avens (*Dryas octopetala*)

Yesterday brought as great a feeling of satisfaction as I believe I can derive from this modern remnant of wilderness. Moments of scenic enchantment were only a portion of the day's profits. I also understood the valley well enough to thread my path upon dry hills and keep out of the tussocks most of the day. I passed features that are unique to areas of high latitudes and they instilled in me a feeling for the ferocity of this environment, which is now merely subdued by the capricious touch of summer. I provided for myself from the stream and soils, taking little enough not to disturb any population or leave behind any scars or remnants of my passing.

I came here to experience wildness, both in the land and in myself. Tests for my motivation and instinct to survive appear constantly. I am independent: I care for myself in every aspect of life or I could not live here now or ever. I see the aspects of tameness that are ingrained in me from my civilized, modernized upbringing. When the going gets difficult, I can always pull from my memory moments and places of easier movement and life-styles, and I curse the difficulties brought upon me by the life-style that I have chosen for these weeks. I can remember days in the Rockies when the country was rugged and wearing. But at times like that I could think, with a car just a few hours away, that my discomforts would soon be cured by a soft cushion, a sandwich, and a ride home. Here and now it is so different. I carry items of necessity and basic comfort, and though they help relieve the necessity to provide constantly for my livelihood, they also produce my discomfort, adding a tremendous load to carry over this tundra, where walking one mile requires the energy of walking two or three or countless more in more usual situations. My pack is the trade-off for my independence. If I carried nothing, or very little, I could move easier, but I would spend much more time daily gathering necessities and slight comforts. Also, I feel that in this wilderness of the 1970s and beyond, the land should not be expected to provide nonnative man with total support. The region is hard-pressed enough by modern man who uses the area; there are few places that would not be badly affected by the intensive use that total self-sufficiency would require.

Lois and Herbert Crisler, who twenty-three years ago spent some time filming caribou and living in several nearby valleys, thought that animals represent the wilderness—without them, the rest is only scenery. When the Crislers saw the area, it was still in its primeval, pristine condition. Much has happened since then, and though the scenery has not been altered, the animals that inhabit the area and migrate through it have suffered the consequences of human encroachment and hunting with the aid of airplanes, snowmobiles, and rifles. So far I have not seen even one caribou though I have been here ten days and traveled over sixty miles, with my senses always on the alert for life. I know I am here at the time when most of the caribou have moved to the north and have not yet started south into the Brooks Range, but I had expected to see stragglers. I know there are still many caribou, and, for some reason, the scarcity of animals does not lessen the feeling of wilderness and remoteness for me as it probably would for the Crislers.

I am slow today. My right foot feels as if a blister is developing on my Achilles tendon. It hurts to walk, and I limp, throwing that leg ahead with each step so I do not put too much pressure on it. I apply moleskin to the area to prevent more rubbing, but it doesn't help. I must be about halfway to the Alatna River, and the thought of limping there is frightening. If this develops into a blister, I am going to be in real pain, and the walk will become more miserable, even if the tussocks disappear.

I cross Agiak Creek for the last time. The water is as cold as I can stand it. I feel as if it is rushing right through my legs. If this stream were over waist-deep, I would be afraid to cross it. The gravel bar along the stream is covered with flowering fireweed, and the pink color is just a bit lighter than that of my legs. I sit on the bank to rest as I dry my feet, then start climbing up the mountainside, following old ruts that wind through meadows and patches of tussocks. The ruts are not deep, and braid back and forth paralleling the river. One meadow is alive with yellow blossoms of vetches, and a pair of caribou antlers protrudes, white and bleached in vertical display. Many caribou once used this valley as a route in crossing these mountains.

Rain sprinkles down now, and I use this as an excuse to rest my sore foot. I build a small shelter with my rain poncho and hide under it. I feel a remoteness that I have not felt so far. I feel I am wasting my time and my life's energy fighting with this country. I do not want to fight with it; I want to learn about it. I want to understand what it will take for man to strike a balance with these mountains and valleys. The change that is overrunning the rest of Alaska and the West should not be allowed to run reckless and further reduce the fragments of wilderness that exist now. It will take an understanding of the natural processes of the area to determine the most feasible methods of integrating human activities into the scheme. Studies here must be initiated now before the impacts become overwhelming; only here does opportunity exist to work with the management of wilderness landscapes because the impacts have not yet become severe. These thoughts stir me; I want to work with these problems. I am experiencing things that people will always want and need to experience in the future.

I break out of my shelter and set off toward the pass that will lead me into Easter Creek. I look across the five or six golden miles of this Agiak Creek basin to a high mountain that rises to the south. It is tall and gray, with a round head and broad shoulders that drop gently to the valley floor. Its face is streaked with ribbons of snow that drain into deep gullies merging toward the creek.

I turn west toward the pass that leads into Easter Creek. Keeping to the base of the mountain and rocky areas, I find spongy meadows dotted with blossoms. I set a good pace now that will net a few miles before the end of the day and fan my hand back and forth at the after-storm mosquitoes. It is always nice to walk just as the storm breaks. There is no glaring sun. The breeze runs across my face and chest, cooling and tingling them as it plucks the drops of sweat from my skin. I cross what must be the pass and head for a small stream that drains from the mountains to the north. The pass here is much like the pass that separates Agiak from Chandler—low, broad, and hardly noticeable. I find it amazing that somewhere on this pass is a line of tussocks where, if I sat there during a rain, I could find the spot where raindrops that fell on one side of the tussock would roll down its side and off toward the Arctic Ocean, and drops on the other side just a fraction of space away would wind their way to the Bering Sea, a thousand miles from the Arctic Ocean. The difference in slope is not apparent to my eye, but surely such a place exists.

I come at last to a small willow forest and the stream bank. The shrubs here are ten feet high, and the plants stand as individuals, with several feet between each. The floor of this forest is covered with luxuriant mosses and spotted with herbs that I am seeing for the first time in these mountains. Monkshood grows in patches, and its tall stems support a handful of brilliant dark blue to purple flowers. I welcome this burst of color. Its few leaves are scattered up and down the stems, each the shape of a hand held out with fingers spread. This is so appropriate because this plant, and many other related species (such as larkspur), are highly poisonous. The welcome yellow flowers of *Senecio* and pink of *Valeriana* are here, too.

I make camp in a beautiful stretch of moss. The ground is damp, but my plastic ground cloth will keep me dry. I dig up a handful of the nutlike bistorts and some coltsfoot, and gather leaves and shoots, until I have a grapefruit-sized pile. I go to the stream to look for fish, but do not even get my line wet—the stream is shallow and braided, running swiftly, and the showers of the afternoon have added enough crumbled earth to the water to turn it brown. I scoop a potful of this muddy water and take it back to camp. Then I get a few rocks and some kindling for a fire. The area is a virtual paradise for the evening. I gather a whole armload of wood and sit down, leaning against the trunk of a handsome willow as I help my fire prepare dinner. In a place like this where the vegetation is a thin veneer, I peel it back intact and build a fire in the exposed area. This way, after cooking, I can toss my rocks into the creek for them to be washed clean of any fire stain, spread out the ashes of fire, and roll back the cover of moss. It leaves the area looking scarcely disturbed when I am gone.

This evening as I slurp a spoonful of muddy-water vegetable soup, I hear a splashing in the creek and look over to see a small bull moose walking down the middle of the stream. He is not in any big rush, and I ask him if he would like some soup. He looks at me, obviously uninterested, and ambles on his chosen path down into the valley. I did not expect to see a moose here, but as I look at the willows, I notice that the tips of many branches are chewed off. I go to the creek and watch him make his way down toward the valley bottom. I get out my binoculars and can see several more moose at Lonely Lake, which sits just at the Continental Divide and drains into Agiak Creek. I wonder whether this is lonely country for moose, too, and if every night they gather by this small body of water just to make sure they are not really isolated. I think how funny it is that no other animals on earth wander off by themselves. They all go places where they can live, and always go with others of their species. Many have their young in these summer areas, but they would not be shocked to see another of their kind anywhere they traveled. I would be shocked to see another of my kind here. I guess most people are just like these animals and stay where there are other people.

It's a clear, content evening, and I want to follow this moose down into the valley to join the other moose, but I know it is too laky down there for my dry-loving body. Anyway, there is an abundance of wood here, and I am eager to dry out my boots. I have not had dry boots since I left the Kollutarak valley five days ago, and it is worth spending several hours to dry them. Putting a stick inside each unlaced boot to keep each one open on a rock near the fire, but not too near, I rotate the boots from side to side. Getting the leather too hot may cause it to crack, and I take no chances of that. Steam sifts out from the insides of the boots, and I smile the whole time, feeling the beginnings of dryness.

Eskimo potato (*Hedysarum alpinum*)

I start early in the morning, moving along the northern part of the valley. The walking is not easy, but I am making good progress. Tussocks are not the major type of vegetation anymore. Instead the terrain is a maze of small hummocks. They are covered with shrubby birches which spread their limbs between hummocks, hiding the fact that the area is not just a smooth carpet of vegetation. Blueberries, Labrador tea, Eskimo potatoes, and willows grow with the birches and mosses. The whole mass is an unstable soft jumble of plant tissue that my steps sink into. The tops of hummocks are pliable and damp. The rims and areas between hummocks are wet, and small tussocks grow there. I walk in huge strides, almost jumping to stay off the higher parts of the hummocks, and away from the lower parts.

Many clouds are floating across the blue sky, and it is the warmest weather I have had so far. I wear only a T-shirt on my upper body, but sweat still pours from me, and I pat my brow almost constantly to keep the sweat from my eyes. The temperature is probably only a bit over seventy degrees Fahrenheit, but walking with this heavy pack across the brush and hummocks is overheating me. The sun is strong and again I feel as if I am in the desert, craving water. There are lots of clouds in the sky, and I would think there would be some relief from this heat, but not one cloud puts itself between me and the sun.

Isolated sections of dry ridges run along this side of the valley, and anytime I can get to one, I walk upon it even though it may mean a climb and a distance of only a few hundred feet. It is a nice change, and provides long open views of the valley and dry places to sit. On these hills I find more new plants. Blue lupines flock in colorful abundance, yellow paintbrush are contrasted against the dark-colored earth. The whole environment is taking on a warmer feeling. It could be the maturation of the summer, but the shrubs are taller everywhere, and there is the addition of another insect that I do not particularly care to deal with—the horsefly. No one told me about horseflies. They are not abundant (and I hope they will not become so), but they are most persistent. I can swat at one of these half-inch-long animals, and it just flies to another part of my body. My shirt has numerous tears in it already, and I am finding that the pressure of my pack against the wet material as I bend and walk is ripping it easily. These flies have no problem finding exposed skin where they can take a luscious bite.

Small streams with banks of willows break up the hummocks and hills, and I rest to take water and cool off. The streamsides are lined with fireweed, and looking up one of these streams is like looking up a series of ribbons—the tall green willows on the banks, pink fireweed paralleling them, and a bright splashing stream running up the middle. These streams and their willows are home for white-tailed ptarmigan, and I scare up small flocks of them everytime I mingle among the willows. Each time, their explosion of flight is unexpected and causes my heart to race in fright. They flush out like pheasants and are gone in an instant, landing among some distant willows where I try to find them but realize I could not find them if I spent all day trying. These birds seem to be mostly males, and the reddish-tinged feathers of their heads flash in the sun as they suddenly bolt from the willows in a gallant escape from intrusion.

The willow and birch shrubs grow tall upon the flanks of hills and I rest here often, crawling under the canopy to crouch in the minute bits of shade cast by these slender-leaved species. Here I am often visited by sparrows that are quite large and darkly colored, with a large spot in the center of a light breast. They are tree sparrows, and their song is made up of loud clear notes, contrasting with the "oodling" of the golden plovers that roam the dry hills.

Whenever my mind is not occupied with walking, it dwells again and again on the increasing pain that grows in my feet. It's not that I'm being physically hampered, it's that I'm being mentally impeded. The thought of crippling blisters and use-less feet frightens me to no end. I think at a bad moment that I can't go on, I'll never make it to the Alatna. But these are the worst of my thoughts, and I quickly swat them away as I do flies and other pests that slow my movement.

I walk hard all day, dining casually and occasionally on my cornmeal-wheat biscuits, smothered with honey. I descend now into the center of the valley to find a suitable place to cross Easter Creek. It is downhill, and the slight bit of pull afforded me by gravity helps lengthen my strides to those of a hurdler bounding over barriers of hummocks. It is about a mile from where I walk on the side of the valley to the creek, but I make short time of it. The creek is inaptly termed. It has been flowing only about ten miles, but the breadth of this valley has donated a vast quantity of water to this riverlike channel. I have a difficult time finding a place that I really care to cross, as it is a meandering stream, slow and deep. I come upon a riffle that scoots rapidly between two deep pools, and I change into my sneakers. I pull up my pant legs and tighten the drawstrings, halfway up my thighs. The insects immedi-ately are on my skin and I do not hesitate to jump into the frigid water.

On the opposite side, I change footgear and start up the hillslope heading southwest toward July Creek. It is still soggy going, and my feet start to drag on the hummocks. I am tired—I should have stopped already—but something pushes me on toward the Alatna, though it is still days ahead. This is the last part of the huge Easter Creek drainage that I will be traversing. The Chandler, and now Easter, are more like basins than valleys. It is miles across them, and there is little gradient in them. Tussocks and hummocks again make walk-ing miserable. I am going through continuous battles with myself to keep moving. If I were with someone, maybe we could make a joke and laugh a little, and know that we both were going through the same struggles. I can remember doing that in high school football practices. The relentless heat of sun, the constant pouring of sweat, the hated drills. I'd think to myself, "What am I doing this for?" Then I'd catch a glimpse of a friend behind his facemask and mouthguard. We would stare into each other's sweat-surrounded eyes and then smiles would grow on our faces, becoming laughter. We knew we were going through it together and the pain immediately vanished.

But I can make no jokes now. Nothing seems funny. Sweat is rolling from every part of my body, and mosquitoes drone around me by the thousands. My pack is bearing down as if it were filled with rocks, and my legs lose their strength as my whole body loses strength, and I sink down onto the rolling hillside.

I turn over onto my back and slink out from the shoulder straps of my pack. I look up at the sky, and as I do, small drops of rain touch down in the birches, splatter against the nylon of my pack, and strike my already wet face. The wind comes up and the chill runs through me, but a quick shiver pushes it away. Rain comes down for real now, and I watch the valley get darker and darker, and I watch myself get wetter and wetter.

I force myself to stand, and dig my poncho out from my pack. I sit on my sleeping bag, lean back on my pack, and drape the poncho over the top of the pile. The rain is coming down hard, and I feel like setting up my tent here, but there is not a flat square foot. I put my head through the hole in the poncho and sit up to watch the rain. The mosquitoes are undaunted by this precipitation and are anxious to feed on my warm blood. I look around for a small, dry hill or flat spot where I can make camp for the night. I see none—just the hummocks and the birches.

The rain slows down and I crawl into my pack, stand up, and start up the hillside. I trudge on for a half mile or so and sit to rest. My pants are soaked from the constant brushing against dripping birches. My misery is complete with water dripping from my nose, and I steep in my depression until I raise my head and gaze across the valley.

It is like no other valley in the world. The waters drain westward, then north joining the Killik, and finally rest in the Arctic Ocean. A storm has just passed through, and its moisture lingers in beads on the birch leaves and as a mist on the cottonlike seed mass of the cotton grass, and its clouds linger on the high peaks to the southwest. As I look north, the valley floor is about a thousand feet below me, with Easter Creek meandering toward the sea. Two miles from me to the north, peaks rise, smooth and flat, rolling at first, then with faces of rock here and there, and then with an abrupt vertical rise into two magnificent mountaintops. One has a small square top, and the other is a perfect cone, graceful, symmetrical, pointed at its summit.

To the east lies the divide between Easter Creek and Agiak Creek, the water from the Agiak side going toward the Pacific Ocean. There are many mountains in this direction, as far as sight allows. Behind me to the south rises a cliffed ridge, low and paralleling the valley. The ridge ends abruptly, and a small tributary comes down from the southwest, the area of the pass that leads to July Creek. The mountains in that direction are big and spectacular, with valleys opening, and more mountains jut up and are silhouetted as far as I can see. To the west lies the most magnificent valley. Nine small lakes sit like dishes of shimmering mercury. Silver is the only shade of light reflected from the veils of sun that try to break through the black sky. The first lakes are about a mile away and some of the more distant ones five or six miles away. The valley stays broad, running into a giant backbone of mountains far in the distance.

The greenness of all this—like the hills of Ireland or the jungles of Panama, where conditions are right for growth—is overwhelming. The green is spread thinly across the valley, contrasted with the gray mountains and the black clouds, and illuminated softly by shafts of light that descend through pierced clouds. The only difference between this green and all other greens is that this variety puts all 365 days of growth into a few short snowless weeks when the sun does not go down. All the tormenting tussocks and hummocks become invisible, hidden behind this vision of serene landscape, and the birds sing away my pains. I am tired after a long day, a long fight with the valleys and with myself. This night I'll sleep in a bog and enjoy it.

Mountain sorrel (*Oxyria digyna*)

I am getting a late start after a restless "night" period. There are bits of sun flashing from the shiny birch leaves, and the whole slope has a spotty appearance as if thousands of tiny mirrors are signaling to me, "Over here; I'm here." I try to keep my elevation constant as I skirt the mountainside. It is hard walking over countless hummocks and I see no relief in the miles ahead. I find diversion in the bright flowers of Labrador tea and other herbs that grow upon the mossy hummocks and am glad to have an endless appreciation of these plants.

I make it across a few miles of hillside and descend to cross the south branch of Easter Creek. I feel like a hurdler again letting gravity tug at my body, and I cooperate by lengthening my stride until I am loping down the hill. My boots squish into the soggy, thick moss cover of the hummocks, and the noise echoes after each step. I count the squishes for awhile, and sing songs.

Soon I am across the slope and down to the creek. I find a shallow riffle where I cross the water, and drop my pack on the other side. The river flood plain is covered with a luxuriant stand of willows that must be ten feet high. The shrubs are spotted here and there on the sandy, gravelly plain. It is calm and dry and hot for a minute, so I strip off my clothing and dash into the creek. This fork of Easter Creek is only about twelve feet across, but at each meander, the water pools up five or six feet deep. I dive into one of these pools. This water is so cold that no matter how hot the human body is, every bit of heat is lost in the very first moments of impact. I surface with the bubbles of my dive and realize that my face has a pained expression all over it. Then I fight with the chill and muster my way out of the water. I get out shivering, and stand there in what bits of sun still shine through the increasingly cloudy sky. I shake my body, and flail my head back and forth to eliminate as much water as I can from my body. I look at my legs, where hundreds of mosquitoes are buzzing around, but not one is landing, as if the cold, wet surface holds no appeal. I am amazed by this and stand there until I dry. Increasing dryness and warmth coming back to my skin surface seem to signal the mosquitoes that it is okay to dig in, so I dress.

The clouds gather up quickly, dark and thick. They push against the mountains, seemingly filling the sky. Soon the heavens must be full because the clouds start building downward, filling the valley. I find a nice willow clump by the stream and drape my rain poncho over a portion of it. I gather myself and all my gear under the shelter, and prepare for the rain, which does not keep me waiting. I don all my clothes as the damp breeze permeates my body. I lie back upon my sleeping bag and munch on a few peanuts, becoming compelled by my shrunken stomach to eat until I feel full. I stop and eat my biscuits with honey, and then resume my peanut devouring. I have eaten few peanuts each day, saving them for a time of dire food need. I see that the need really is a psychological rather than a physical one. I stare off across the misted valley into the clouds.

Loneliness comes like a wave now, completely overwhelming me. I take out the only photograph that I carry and look at each of the smiling faces of my family gathered around the hearth. I feel that they are here with me, or that I am there with them a million miles away. I close my eyes and talk with each of them, and I cry, happy to know that soon I can be with them. It is a crazy thing—being alone and wishing and dreaming that I really am not alone. I wonder if my imagination is what enables me to maintain my motivation and my stability. I can put myself in any place that I want to be, live it for awhile, and return to my life here, in the Brooks Range, partially relieved. A bit of vicarious love is better than nothing at all.

It rains for a few hours and I lounge around eating peanuts until I feel I could burst. I lie down for awhile, then sit up to read and write for awhile. I hear a low-pitched quack and look out from under my shelter to the creek. A single female red-breasted merganser is swimming in the calm pool that runs in front of my feet. She quacks and swims in small circles, all the time looking around as if she has lost something. I find it curious that she has appeared all of a sudden like this, alone. Maybe she has been upstream, and has merely ridden the current downriver to keep me company. Maybe she has lost track of her brood and is searching for them. She stays in the same pool for an hour or so. I would invite her in out of the rain if I knew that she would be fond of peanuts and my company.

The rain slackens and ceases sometime later in the afternoon, and I am chilled as the wind picks up. The cloud-enclosed valley gives the intensified impression that it is really cold here. I get up to gather some wood for a fire. The sandy ground is not wet, as the rain has not pooled here. The willows are dripping, and all dead branches are sopping. I gather a bunch of medium-thick branches and split them lengthwise with my sheath knife. This exposes what dry wood there may be. All bits of kindling are totally useless. I strip off shavings of wood and order it into a small tepee raised upon a few cross members of wet wood. I put a match under this, and watch the smoke rise and drift away. I lay my face to the ground and add lung power to the task. More oxygen always helps the fire get started. Fire is slow at coming this day, however, and it is several minutes, several matches, and a lot of blowing before there is any sort of a blaze. Once I get it going, I build it up to get some coals and heat to warm my hands and spirit. I burn twig after twig, and bathe in their heat and smoke. I cook up a small portion of cornmeal mush, mix in a spoonful of honey, and let them slide down my esophagus to warm up my innards.

The sky breaks just enough to show light gray and occasional blue, which sets me to traveling again. I walk along the sandy riverbanks where I can, but as the main fork branches east, I branch west across the wet hummocks covering the tundra. I walk on for a few hours, soaked from mid-thigh down to my toes, and the sky gets almost black and streaks of rain descend onto mountains beyond my sight. It clears to gray, and a stiff wind bends the branches and wipes the drops of moisture from glossy leaves. There are a few dry hills along the sides of this valley, and I take the time to rest.

I walk a few grueling miles in all, and then come upon a small group of crystalline rocks, which jumble the landscape and produce raised strips of turf. I choose one of these to set my shelter upon. I build a small fire from birch twigs, and, as I measure out the water for my rice, I realize that I have run out of water. All of this rain, all of this soggy ground and dripping foliage, and I have no water to drink. I look upon the rocks and find two small depressions where small amounts of water have accumulated. I spoon the fluid into my water bottle, and clutch it as if it were treasure. I realize the importance of camping along streams, something I have taken for granted all other days.

I see now that walking is such a rugged thing, especially for my mind. I always must press onward, onward, and it wrings my muscles of their sweat and my mind of its appreciation of my surroundings. If I ever make it out of these mountains, I know I will be back again, but next time it will be accompanied, and I will stay near a main camp for several days and explore the area from that position. It would relieve the strain of constantly carrying the hundred-pound pack and the daily task of finding a camp, food, and water, and thereby make it easier to do what I really wanted to do in the first place— enjoy and know the Brooks Range. On this trip, I am pushing myself to the maximum. Interspersed with the pain and suffering are moments of peace, inexpressible beauty, and tranquillity. I am experiencing these mountains in their most brutal character (though not in the most brutal season), and am learning why they are still so remote: it is really tough to travel in and out of them on foot. Snowshoeing or skiing in winter would be easier, as the tussocks and hummocks would be covered with snow.

I lie upon an island in a sweltering sea of confused landscape. Bog birches are thick everywhere along with willows. Add a layer of moss six inches deep, tussocks of cotton grass and sedge, blueberry shrubs, Labrador tea, coltsfoot, reindeer lichens, and a trillion mosquitoes, and you've got where I'm at with no back door—only one way out of it and that's through it. And from here I can see five more miles of the same. For tonight I'll sleep in a bog. Could anything be finer?

American golden plover

July 18

I start up through the gaping pass that leads to the head-
waters of July Creek. I am full of energy this morning, and feel
as if I am charging up this hummocked hillside in anticipation
of the approaching Continental Divide and drainage change.
The top of this pass is indefinite, as are the tops of most of the
passes in this part of the range. The view changes slightly, and
I can feel my body rejoice as it senses the beginning of descent.

There is a small lake at the head of the July Creek valley,
and the stream emerges from the body of water. I walk from
the hillside onto the sandy flood plains, and leave the hummocks to themselves up on the hillsides. There are lots of
willows, a new shrub called shrubby cinquefoil, and blueberries and fireweed. It is dry and unobstructed, so I easily
make good progress. I look at the water and I tell it, "You and
I, we're both going to the same place."

The stream is tiny here, two or three feet wide on the
average, and in one swift deep spot, much narrower. I sit to
drink some water at one of these deep areas, and notice four
huge grayling lazily keeping their position in the current.
They rise now and then for some floating material that I
cannot see, but otherwise do little moving. I wonder what it is
like for these fish during the long winters. A stream this small
must be very severe when there is little flowing water, little
food, and lots of cold days. Maybe they move back up into
the lake for the winter. Walking along the stream and mingling hillsides is now offering me another challenge, for
nestled among the verdure are carefully camouflaged green
berries. They are crunchy, juicy, not very flavorful, though
certainly abundant. I sit whenever I come to a patch of these
fruits and wish that I could hurry the season to the day when
these will ripen into blueberries. I miss fresh fruit, and the
taste of these berries enlivens these urges even more. The one
food I did not bring enough of is dried fruit, and it is all but

gone. I also have cravings for dairy products—Colby cheese on freshly baked bread or a tub of rich yogurt. At times like these I mix up a thick cup of powdered milk. I chew up the lumps, and let my tongue stir the substance around my mouth. The sweet taste of the whole milk blossoms then, and I am utterly satisfied until the same thoughts come again.

Downstream a few miles after many small tributaries have nourished July Creek into a decent-sized body of water, I stop for some sport fishing. The stream is cutting a small canyon out of sedimentary bedrock and creates a lush environment, with willows reaching tree size and form. The stream leaps from pool to glorious pool. I opt for roll casting instead of overhand because the vegetation grows too near the stream-side and snags my line and fly on a backcast. My casting is far from graceful or perfect, but it doesn't matter. The grayling are interested in anything I throw out, and any way that I throw it out. I catch and release fish for about a half hour and finally a cast drifts the length of the pool without enticing any more takers. I figure that I have caught and released most every fish in this neck of the stream, so I pack up and move on.

The valley now opens to the northwest, where another fork of this river comes down from the mountains to join July Creek. At the junction the river turns and heads straight south, and takes on the name Kutuk. This junction is a most lovely spot, with green mountains on every side, a rushing stream, a handful of puffball mushrooms to put into my dinner pot, a strong sun, and clouds that look like they would love to rain on me.

I make it about halfway to the junction of Coalit Creek to the south before stopping for the evening. This valley is not steep and spectacular, but green and wild. It gives me the feeling of comfort. A flat, well-drained spot overlooks the river and entices me to camp for the evening. A wind comes from some distant thundershower, and funnels down this flumelike valley. The mosquitoes are absent for the moment, and I venture to the river to fish. The river is braided, and has a huge rocky flood plain, bare of vegetation. The water is shallow and swift in almost every stretch, and I find one fish that could not be even four inches in length. I send him home to bring back his big brother, but they do not return. I wish now that I had kept a few fish from this afternoon's sporting.

I gather an armload of wood from the abundant stands of willows and build a small fire. The evening environment brings a calm, and the smoke wafts unhurriedly down the valley. I gather an extra dose of roots to make up for the absence of fish in my diet. While rooting in the nearby hills, I come upon a small patch of an exquisite pinkish paintbrush. I look upon the mountainside spotted with clumps of willows and, combined with the feeling drawn upon me by the paintbrush, I feel as if I am in southwestern Colorado during springtime in some hills covered with piñon junipers. But here there are no trees. The ground is frozen an arm's length below my feet. This is tundra, produced by the cool temperatures and shortness of the growing season, the continuous light of the growing season, and the continuous dark and cold of the nonsummer seasons. And yet, this valley gives me the feeling of warm southern climates. The low, dry mountains are bare of soils or vegetation on their ridges and summits. The large, barren, braided flood plain of the Kutuk, the shrubby, almost scrubby appearance of the tallest vegetation, are most reminiscent of desert mountains.

I stir my mushroom soup with a green willow switch and add a heaping spoonful of margarine for richness. Puffballs are plentiful here, but they are not one of the more flavorful of wild mushrooms. In this situation, however, who is choosy? I guess that being in my present position—ninety to a hundred miles from the village of Anaktuvuk and twenty to thirty from the Alatna River and about two hundred from Allakaket or Kobuk—eating mushrooms is a foolish and overly dangerous thing to do. Any type of poisoning could be fatal, or at least could hinder my ability to walk out of here. I never really dwell on the possibility, however, and have a bagful of puff-ball mushrooms either fried or in my soup every evening that I can find them.

This evening as I am slurping a spoonful of soup, I happen to look up the hillside to my right. The spoon drops out of my hand and my mouth drops open, letting the soup run down my chin. About 150 yards up the hill, the largest bear I have ever seen is galloping down the mountainside directly toward me. I think it must be a grizzly, but its coat of deep black shines in the sun and I realize it is a black bear. I am paralyzed. The hillside is a jumble of hummocks, and the ease with which it gallops across the terrain is startling—its form is fluid, its motion effortless. I could never outrun this animal. It stops for a moment, lifts its head to sniff the air and obviously smells something. I wonder, remembering how poor a bear's eyesight is, if it has any idea where I am. On down it comes and lopes about thirty yards away, disappearing into the tall shrubbery along the river without even looking at me. I sit still for about five minutes and wonder about the certain death that has just waltzed by. I wasn't petrified, but damned near. I get up and walk toward the river where the bear had departed. Its tracks are scattered between the rocks along the river and head upstream to locations I have no desire to discover.

I walk back to camp, build up my fire again, and reheat my soup. The thoughts of my perilous position soon vanish, and I reflect on the amazing ability of that animal to move in this country. How well equipped it is for life here.

One great thing about tundra is that when you see an animal, you have an unobstructed view for the minutes or seconds it takes for it to pass across your field of vision. It is nice that I have such a clear view; animal occurrences are rather rare.

The skies clear, becoming cloudless this evening. I sit around the fire extra long tonight, as the unlimited amount of wood allows. I look about the valley and upon my situation, and with a sense of humor I say to myself, "A clear night—I guess I'll go camping."

The valley is mysterious this morning, and I am filled with thoughts of bears, remoteness, and unfamiliar country. The sky is overcast with dark threatening clouds, and my horizons are shaded gray in every direction. I mix some powdered milk with my granola and spoon in a small amount of river water to liquefy the mass. I eat slowly, and the sugars churn in my mouth, burning my throat. When the ration is gone, I walk to the river, lie on my belly, and drink deeply. The water rids my mouth of the sugars and bits of oat flakes, replacing them with the chilled freshness that these mountains pour forth. Rolling over to my back, I feel the water taking my hair away and pushing at my whole head. Looking up at the gray sky and around at the green hills and shaly cliffs, I detect no movement, just the timelessness of the life in this valley, the timelessness of the river that forever passes through and forever stays in this valley. Sometimes my life seems as infinite as the birches or willows that constantly sprout new forms from spreading rhizomes, and roots that reach out to encompass new and richer earth. If I were to stay here for the rest of my life, I could cover this whole valley, not by roots but certainly on foot and within my mind. But now I feel so finite, as if all the minutes of my days could be spent here, while the valley lived on long after I died, with some of its life-forms taking nourishment from me. Life would go on, pushed by time, flowing as the ribbon of water flows around my form, and I would live, and I would die—unknown, unheard, unseen by anyone but myself.

I gather my gear and start down the Kutuk. Along the river are the first scattered clumps of alders, which add a dense, thick character to the vegetation. The presence of alders is a response to this warmer, more southerly climate. Because it forms thickets, the alder has changed many of the environment's features and the fauna inhabiting these groves are distinct from the fauna of the rest of the area. Here birds that I have not seen thus far are present. Varied thrushes nest in the alders and fill the air with their boisterous reports and dashing chases. Wilson's and arctic warblers flit in the scrubs at streamside. White- and golden-crowned sparrows are everywhere in the vegetaton and small accumulation of rocks along the stream.

I sit and watch the birds, which are pioneers of their species, for here they are at the utter extreme of their habitable environment. How finite their environment is. From their southern winter homes they wing as far as the very last alder shrub where the boreal forest succumbs to the tundra environment. Country to the north is home to tundra plants and birds. Here the birds I study have colonized every shrub of alder, and there are no more nesting territories, no more unexplored valleys, no more uninhabited parts of the globe. All the possible niches in this riparian environment are filled. There are a finite number of nests, a finite number of young born each year, and thus their populations are limited by space and resources. How slow humans are to adopt these ways. Or, maybe how sly humans are, able to extract greater resources from environments with the aid of technology.

I continue down the Kutuk and cross the river before the confluence with Coalit Creek. Open grassy meadows sprawl on south-facing slopes, and I can walk along and not worry about the positioning of my feet with each step. I have spans of whole minutes where I can look at the country. I feel relaxed in movement, my stride long and unhesitant, my mind stimulated by and discerning of all that I view. Much of the pain that has built up in me for the past two weeks is quickly hidden. The tussocks are gone for the most part, thanks to better slope drainage. It is so exhilarating to be here, and now that I am comfortable, it seems as if I have been here before. Maybe this is how I have always dreamed it would be in the wilderness—unending expanses of valleys and mountains, continuously enchanting pristine landscapes, with time and steady walking pace the only requisites to enjoyment. Almost all of the country that I have crossed thus far has been nothing like this image, but now I get a taste of it, a dream realized. How odd that I can let these fleeting pleasures overwhelm me so, when alternative minutes are bathed in pain. I guess I am looking for real, feeling experiences, and when it comes as pleasure, I take it in with all my heart.

The Kutuk makes a bend to the east and takes on a braided character. I cross it again to walk on the assorted rocks and gravel that line the river on the outside of the bend. River beauty is the only plant growing in this naked environment and adds splendid splashes of green leaves and pink blossoms to the gray shades of alluvium. The valley walls are interrupted by many gullies and channels. The gullies are marked by a cut in the steep valley wall and a broadening fan of alluvium spreading down to the river. Alder seems to have a special affinity for these alluvial fans, because it grows on them in thick, continuous stands. An individual alder will grow to about twelve feet in height, sending thick branches vertically and horizontally from every level of its stems. The shrubs grow close together, with branches from one individual mingling with those of its neighbors. The result is a fiercely tangled layer of vegetation that poses incredible problems in walking because it extends from the valley wall down to the river's edge. Here on the outside of this bend in the river, the water has eroded into the flood plain right up to the bases of a stand of alder. It has produced a cutbank that is about five vertical feet from the ground surface to the water surface, and here the water is quite deep and swift. I find myself putting my head down, trying to plow through the alder thickets, but branches over three inches in diameter do not bend at all. I must bend my body to fit the shapes of the gaps between the branches, and over the branches. In some places, there is no way but on my belly, and in others I find myself several feet off the ground walking from branch to branch. My pack and my bow catch on everything, and it is a constant fight to tear them from the grasp of the alder.

I try to walk on the very edge of this cutbank, holding the

branches and hanging back away from them, finding footing on branches on the edge of the bank. Many times I lose my footing and dangle momentarily above the river. It requires a tremendous amount of work to make a hundred yards, but there are moments of extreme beauty in the middle of these thickets. A small plant, *Boschniakia rossica,* which is a root parasite on the alder, looks like a purple pine cone. Willows also add unusual color to the ground. In some places the alder is so thick that I can't even see my feet through all the leaves. Surrounded by lush green with squawking birds and dashing forms in the brush that I hear but never see, I feel as if I am in a jungle. Happily not all the walking is like this, because it would take me all day to make one mile. There are long stretches of grassy, sedgy meadows with dry, firm footing and little vertical confusion at the ground level. I pick up a stout branch of an alder and use it as a cane to take a bit of the weight of walking from the foot that is still troubling me. At times I feel as if I am in the park on Sunday tooling along the path and sodded grasses. I look to the vegetation, I look to the birds, I look to these mountains. "Ah, it's a fine day to be here."

The clouds build up many times this day, spitting a few drops of rain, then pulling back and moving on. Toward evening the rains come for real and I hastily build my tent on a beautiful high river bar where the sands are as fine as those on a California beach. I walk barefooted and take a vacation. I piece together my fly rod and run to the river to try to capture a fish for my pot. There are some promising pools, and I wade out into the river, fishing behind rocks, along cliff walls, and in the backs of pools. No luck. Not even a nibble from a grayling. I gather an armful of alder branches from a nearby stand and start a fire among some larger rocks near my sandbar. The rain is coming down lightly, and I huddle over the fire as its branches of flame reach up to warm my hands and face. My rain poncho has been set up as my shelter, so I roll up the collar of my wool shirt and roll down the earflaps of my old cotton duck cap, and let the rain touch down on my body. It is not long before the boiling mass of rice and roots is tender. I add two heaping spoonfuls of margarine and a pinch of salt, fry up my biscuits for lunch tomorrow. I throw all of the hot, fire-smudged rocks into the river to be cooled, cleaned, and forgotten. I crawl into my sleeping bag, strip off my clothing, and push most of it into the foot of my bag. My wet wool shirt I lay alongside my bag, to be dried in the morning if the sun shines. My soup is quickly slurped down, and its warmth satisfies my cold, damp body. I curl up inside my sleeping bag and shiver for awhile to heat up the environment that it encases. All is quiet but for the rain hitting my tent and the sand.

Long-tailed jaeger

It rains all night, and as the sky lightens with morning, it rains harder. I roll in my bag, restless to awaken and, at the same time, relieved that it is not yet time to be up. The sands under my body have compacted into a solid layer that rivals the firmness of glacially polished granite. Clouds are low in the valley, with fragments hanging to the floor. I have my granola inside my shelter with me and chase it down with water. The rain slows to a drizzle, then ultimately stops. Clouds shrink and become more remote. I crawl from my bag, happily removed from my forced supine posture. The light from the sun is dim at first, but grows strong, filtering through the saturated valley and atmosphere. I find a willow nearby and hang my wet shirt to dry in the humid breeze. Sitting on a rock, I listen to the symphony of drainage—single drops, small gullies, the swollen river. I am in no hurry this morning.

In due time, gravity has pulled the moisture from the vegetation and I resume travel. At about eighteen hundred feet above sea level, I come upon a most welcome sight: a stand of conifer trees, white spruce at timberline. I stop about a quarter mile from the stand and survey its gross features. Surprisingly, this first group of trees is made up of tall, healthy individuals with many small, more youthful members mixed in, giving me the impression that this stand is firmly established. Forty years ago, Bob Marshall had hypothesized that timberline in the Endicott Mountains was advancing up the valleys, moving higher in elevation and farther north. This stand certainly shows no signs of being at the limit of environments that will support its growth. Possibly, if given a long enough period of time without another ice age, spruce will cover much larger portions of the Brooks Range.

I hike closer to the stand, which is on the other side of the river, and from my high vantage point on a ridge across the way, I notice a small yellowish spot just at the edge of the stand along the river. I train my binoculars on the motionless object and discover that it has a head. I sit down to watch, and the small object gets up and walks into the forest. I know lynx are rarely seen in the summer, and I wish I had several days to keep track of its movements.

The air now also has a beautiful perfume. Balsam poplar is found with the spruce stands and along the watercourses. It has the luxuriant scent of balsam, which radiates from the thick, sticky leaves, and I am immediately fond of it. The trees also provide shade, with high branches and leaves, and their taller form lends to the production of poplar forests that line the river. The trees are twenty to thirty feet high with a six-foot-high layer of willows growing below them. I not only have difficulty seeing and walking through them, but also hear things crashing away through the brush, and I have "daymares" about rousing a grizzly bear and stimulating a hideous reaction. Most of these sounds are too soft to be made by a bear. I scare a moose, which bounds up through the willows, crosses the river, and bawls at me, expressing his fear and anger. I bawl right back at him.

The spruce forests are providing me with great delight as I look at all the new species of shrubs and herbs that have accompanied the spruce on their journey into these mountains. Besides willows and alders, I find shrubby cinquefoil, kinnikinnick, alpine azaleas, crowberries, and alpine blueberries, plus horsetails, mosses, and huge expanses of reindeer lichens. It is lush understory that provides soft, spongy walking. The crowberries (*Empetrum nigrum*) are common, and their small black berries are ripe and juicy. They are not great tasting, but some of the berries are quite good, and I constantly gather handfuls to satisfy my fruit desires. Another small plant, bearberry (*Arctostaphylos rubra*), is in full fruit, and its red, juicy berries dot the forest floor. I pick few of these as they are tasteless, though bears eat large quantities of them. Berries are a welcome addition to my diet, both for nutrition and for variety.

Another spruce tree is found along the river in wetter sites. Called black spruce, it is more yellow than the dark green white spruce that inhabit the preferred well-drained slope habitats. White spruce are found higher up on the mountainside, especially on slopes that face south. This exposure produces a warmer site, ameliorating the coldness of the region, and allows the trees on these slopes to grow at a higher elevation. The stands of trees are not continuous, and there are grassy interludes that allow easy movement and a strolling gait.

Evening is splendid, with clearing skies, tinges of purple cloud cover, and a roaring fire. It is such a treat to sit in one spot in a forest and just reach up to overhanging dead limbs and break off what I need to keep my fire going. It seems like a luxury compared with a week ago when I had to hunt for elusive twigs among the tussocks and hummocks of the tundra. Here I can be a fire baron as the amount of dead branches and small dead trees is almost endless. The fire warms me as no flame has warmed me thus far on the trip. I huddle around it, then lay my sleeping bag next to it, watching the swirling orange coals before I fall asleep beneath the gray blue sky, beside warm graying ashes.

I am up and away quickly this morning, with a sense of urgency in my stride. It is not that I am moving rapidly (the forest and riverside prohibit that), but there is no hesitation after each step. I feel as if I could spend the rest of my life walking in this valley, and I must get out of it soon. From a ridge that runs parallel to the valley and several hundred feet higher, I look downriver. A mountain on the left flank juts to the river a few miles ahead. A mountain on the right flank juts to the river a few miles beyond that, and my sight is a series of great bends and mountains, the pattern of which seems unending. In days past, I have made a distance of two or three of these mountains or bends each day. Now looking upriver to country already traveled, I see the backside of familiar mountains. It is a strange feeling to walk in one direction, because all that I look at and come to know turns a different cheek to me as I pass, as if to rob me of the intimacy I have created. No matter how much I look, when I turn to look again, it is not the same. Little intimacy is possible with any mountain, just as with the continuum of change and time.

The forest is broken here and there with trees yielding to birch-covered hummocks and tussocks. These are usually in small depressions, wetter areas where a thick moss cover develops to keep summer's warmth from reaching the soil. Permafrost is closer to the ground surface here, creating even poorer drainage. I usually avoid these wet sites, but I am discovering that blueberries, ripe and swollen with the sweet purple juices that I crave, are growing on green mother plants that top the tussocks and hummocks. I am hopelessly addicted, and I brave the soggy ground to gather this delicacy of the boreal forest. I hate to walk by even a single berry that stares up at me from the forest floor, and I find myself bending over and picking madly, completely oblivious to the weight of my pack. Time after time, I pool the gathering of both hands into one and with a quick swipe send the harvest funneling into my anxious mouth. I smile a shallow smile so as not to interrupt the processes of chewing the succulent fruits, then as soon as the smashed mass is en route to my stomach, my eyes search out another offering. I become swollen with the land, the sun, the products and givings of life. I feel this forest, this valley, every shrub, plant, and mite.

I eat until I am exhausted by the labors of eating. Hoisting my pack, I start off downvalley. I wonder if it is possible for me to walk on a hillside, look to the earth, see scads of bright purple ripeness, and keep right on going. The presence of this fruit has not yet become ordinary to me, and every sighting seems like a first. Even when I am filled with blueberries and not craving their taste, I still feel pulled to the shrubs and I fear that I may cover fewer miles each day. As I move farther down the valley, and deeper into the boreal forest, the blueberry bushes get larger and more common, and the berries get more ripe. In well-drained areas, the forest also is dotted with three other types of ripe, colorful berries: bearberries, buffalo berries, and crowberries. Shades of red, black, and blue add splashes of color to the continuous green and brown of the forest floor. But, there ain't nothin' like blueberries.

I round a hill near mid-day and on its steep, west-facing slope get my first view of a group of peaks that inspires and recharges me with the same magnetic force that has drawn man to explore mountains and pulls them to their summits. Many miles away yet are high, projectilelike, steep, smooth-sided spires of the granite Arrigetch Peaks. I can see a whole ridge of swooping peaks, sharp at the top, piercing the air. I stop and point my binoculars at the pinnacles and find myself unable to look at anything else. My heart beats faster and my mind soars with the mountains. I do not question why these configurations of granite can so change my thought pattern and redefine my motivations and needs. It feels good now to be strengthened by the aura of superbly carved rock. I feel again as I have always thought I would in wilderness — deriving my motivations from the landscape, feeding on it, and not constantly fighting the craving to communicate with other humans.

A new flowering plant, death camas (*Zygadenus elegans*), now is present in the forest. I pity the poor immigrant looking for wild roots who digs it up, for as the name implies, it is deadly poisonous. It is a large plant with showy, yellowish, lilylike flowers that are always attractive.

Days are warm in this lower part of the Kutuk valley. Lugging my pack along the winding river, through crowded spruce forest and balsam-scented riparian strips, causes me great discomfort from sweating. My clothing is soaked with perspiration, and I continually pat my brow with a handkerchief to keep the fluid from dripping into my eyes. The temperature is around seventy degrees Fahrenheit, and it is perfect for sitting and relaxing, though too hot for vigorous movement. I walk along the river, and the sounds of spilling, rushing, cool water make me throw down my pack and clothing and plunge into the river. I always feel so hot before entering one of these rivers that I can never imagine how cold the water really is. My skin shrinks a few sizes, goose bumps soar to new heights, and I scream. I am up like a rebounding spring, shaking, spinning, and doing all manner of things to drive the water from my saturated skin. My spray chases away the insects, but they are back in a moment, and I run to the riverbank and pull on my pants. My T-shirt is still wet with perspiration, and I put on my wool shirt so the cotton can dry in the sun for a little longer.

Downstream the river cuts a miniature canyon and slows into a series of long, deep pools. I grab my fishing rod, attach a favorite black gnat, and head for the nearest pool. I fish from the sandbars that run along the riverside, throwing out long casts that lie across the crystal clear, green-tinged water like a fine white thread. I have no rises, see no grayling, but this does not stop me from fishing, for it is pleasure from the arching, whipping pole that I seek. I love the coiling and un-coiling line lighting on the placid, eddying water, and the an-ticipation and constant prayer that accompany the hook as it floats on the fluid. I turn and walk back along the sandbar and casually glance down to the soft, fine-grained sands. I notice that my footprints are not the only marks in the sand. Terror strikes me like a club, and I wheel around, eyes wide, searching in all directions. The tracks are huge, with marks made by long claws, obviously belonging to the landlord of the valley, a grizzly bear.

In the presence of a larger, stronger animal, I feel stalked and vulnerable and isolated in a different way now. I realize how finite and fragile the union of my mind and body is and wonder why I take the chance that I have to be here. I think about death. Is what I am gaining worth the chance of losing my life?

Thoughts of bears, my broken body, and the seeping away of my mind and life's energy are again put as far away as I can push them. I try to feel the homeyness the flood plain forest offers on this beautiful day. Soon I am walking without listening for soft, stalking steps in the forest around me and am thinking of how I should continue this trip. I had originally planned to reach the village of Kobuk and now, also, have the potential of floating the Alatna River to Allakaket. The sight of Arrigetch Peaks has spawned new strength in my legs and the forces that guide them. I decide to continue on to Kobuk via the Reed River.

Streamside gravel and rounded stones are brought by the water from many parts of this valley. It is uneven walking, and I cannot set a pace because large stones must be negotiated. In other places, there is sand where I can move briskly and smoothly. The Kutuk flow is braided. Strands of water form a twisted maze upon alluvium, and I walk on all substrates, both solid and liquid. There are many tributaries to cross. They are small, whooshing flows of water that have descended from a small side valley or basin cut into the ridges above. Some are but a trickle, gurgling between large rocks in channels formed by much larger flows. The tiny amount of water seems out of place, and I know snow beds are waning. For the rest of the warm season, this area will have flowing water only after rains. Other tributaries are already dry, and no water moves at the surface of their channels. A myriad inputs course toward the Kutuk, each different in size, origin, and streamside array of shrubs and rocks. There is usually a thick band of willows and alders along the banks that I wrestle while crossing. These shrubs grow to their maximum strength and size along these streams.

Infinite courses could be followed by a traveler moving down the valley. Decisions on where to route my body and where to place my steps are made in a never-ending process. I start up the slope, cross grassy patches of meadow and areas of bountiful tussocks, and reach a high ridge covered by spruce. I stop in an open spot where a steep cliff drops straight to the river below me. I dangle my legs over the edge and look down to the Kutuk and up to the steep mountains and high cliffs across the valley. A sharp-shinned hawk circles above, swooping and rising, changing the circumference of its path with every round of flight. I train my binoculars on the bird as it lands momentarily on the cliff and flies again, rising into a speck and disappearing into the blue sky. I pull some ripe berries from a nearby bush and munch them slowly, savoring their flavor.

I have learned two things about myself. I have the mental and physical capacities to walk this vast land of mountains and valleys carrying an enormous load with consistent strength that could breach any mountain range. I watch the sharp-shinned hawk reappear, circling high above the valley. It lands again on the cliffs that rim the northern side of the valley, then flies off bathed in the blueness of Brooks Range morning skies. More importantly now, sitting back at the edge of the clearing in the forest, I realize how I appreciate this country the most, and when I derive the maximum amount of understanding from what I see. It is when I slow down, when I stop and am with the land. When do I see moose and bear, and when do I have the opportunity to watch them as they proceed in their normal ways? When do I enjoy the flight of a hawk or the darting of a grayling or the succulence of a blueberry or the symmetrical petals of summer blossoms? When I am still and observant.

When I think back on the happier moments of this trip, I come up with a new plan. I will take my time, finish walking down the Kutuk to the Alatna, build a raft, do some exploring into Arrigetch for several days, and then float down the Alatna River. I will try to understand my surroundings instead of just seeing country, making miles, and getting out of these mountains. I believe it will be a much more fulfilling visit that way. It is never too late to see things differently, and knowing what I want to get out of this trip, it is the only way to proceed toward fulfilling that goal. The tussocks have fought with me, and I have defended myself by walking swiftly through the valleys that are their home. Here the country is not so aggressive; I need not be constantly on my guard and can focus attention on other features of the area.

The forest is more open in this segment of the valley, and along the bank near the stream are trails that are obviously well kept and maintained. The paths are about one foot wide with very little erosion to deepen the grooves in the landscape.

These trails follow the river, and on one side of the river there are usually several trails that join, then separate, and pick their own way through the maze of forest and clearing, rock and bog. I think that whatever is responsible for these paths must use them frequently, as they are smooth, with few new plants cluttering the exposed brown earth, few roots to trip upon, and with most of the branches from overhanging and low-growing trees and shrubs broken off. I judge from the size of the path and the height to which branches are broken off that these surely must be the paths of moose. But moose are not common in this part of the valley, and I doubt that there were times when they were much more abundant than today. The multitude of trails braiding back and forth in the forest and flood plain suggests that large numbers of animals travel here at the same time. These must be trails of caribou from migrations between the Alatna valley and Easter Creek to the Killik River or Chandler Lake.

I stop and look around and have a dreamlike feeling that the woods are coming alive with movements of caribou. I lean against a spruce tree, and the herds file by, walking along the meandering, mixing trails. Dust is kicked up by scuffing, trampling feet. Just ahead all the animals cross the stream and resume their movement on the other side. I can see, hear, and smell them. But looking around, I see only remnants, memories left behind, and I envision their life passing.

Lower in the valley, the Kutuk turns into a real sidewinder, meandering and cutting deeper into the steep canyon that it has already made for itself. Every turn of the river brings a cliff, the steep mountainsides above densely covered with stands of spruce and birches. Blueberries grow on the hummocks, with knee-high tussocks in the less well-drained pockets. The other side of the river is an open stand of white spruce that is fine for walking. The steep side is too dense for easy and profitable travel, so I find myself stopping to cross the river every time it decides to make a bend in its course. At first I take my boots off, put on my tennis shoes, cross the river, and then boot up again. But soon I see that I will spend the whole day changing footwear and decide to stick with tennis shoes, although they provide very little protection for walking. I cross the river about twenty times today because it is easier to walk on flat gravel bars and in the open spruce stands than to climb over the cliffs among the thick vegetation.

I believe that today is a success. I believe that I've done it, eaten one million blueberries in one day. I can hear the branches sigh in relief as I pull the heavy berries from their branched backs, and I know that I am doing these shrubs a great favor by helping them to stand once again straight and tall.

Large stands of horsetails grow in disturbed areas of slides or drowned forest, and the light green cover of this vegetation is striking against the dark purples, grays, and black clouds that storm in gallant form farther up the valley. Rain streaks across the sky, and the constant flashes of lightning and low, distant rumbling of thunder make me happy that the clouds are not coming downvalley.

It is a weary day, and after yesterday's great spurts of energy after the first sights of the Arrigetch Peaks, I feel as if I have no umph today. I am slow and take occasional pleasure at casting flies into the deep pools of the river, but still without finding any fish. This is slightly disheartening as I have eaten only vegetable matter for days. I had thought that I would have no problem supplying fish for myself every day, and now I am finding it impossible. However, I don't feel a real craving for the meat of grayling; and knowing the needs of my body, I am surprised and happy to find that I am able to stay as healthy as I do with only the grains I carry, the roots I dig, and the berries I pick.

Sometimes I find myself craving bread, something solid, but I have no grains or flour to eat between meals. I have learned the trick of combining a large amount of water with my meals to add volume and satisfy my stomach's need for large quantities of things, but I cannot fool my stomach. Even though I am quite healthy, it thinks I am starving.

I wonder why there are no fish in this portion of the river.

Perhaps there is a small outcrop of rock in the valley that leaches out too much of a specific metal or mineral into the river, killing the invertebrate fauna that is the fish's food source, and thereby eliminating fish.

Dining this evening at the side of the river, I observe a stunning metamorphosis. The water has been smooth, flowing, and crystal clear for all the days that I have walked by its side. But now it begins to run faster. There is a dramatic increase in the amount of water, and it turns brown, running thick and swollen with the easily eroded shales of these mountains. I take a little higher position on the bank and continue slurping my vegetable soup. The water becomes roily, with the foaming white accenting the muddy color. The volume doubles or triples in a short span of time. The rains up the valley during the day have made their water the water of the river; the energy of each drop of rain has made the sediments of the mountain the sediments of the river.

Alatna mañana.

The lower Kutuk continues as a winding river. Its curves are broad, its water deeper and more powerful than any other part of its length. It is also a magnificent canyon, cut through whitish gray limestone that forms cliffs. I try hiking up in the forest, but the slope is steep, wet with lots of alders and willows, and I have to fight. In the canyon, I walk on gravel bars, and, as before, I must cross the river whenever it presents a cliff on my side. Crossing in riffles to other bars, I stir up sand and mud that move with the water into my shoes. On the gravel bars, the water runs out and the sand is left stranded in my sneakers to rub against my bare, tender skin. I feel as if they are lined with sandpaper. I walk anyway, with stiffer feet and unflexing ankles, to minimize abrasion and to eliminate the need to change footgear all day long.

I find a stout pole to help brace myself as I place each step in the swift water. There are lots of flies here. In midstream one always finds a dry spot on my neck or the back of my thighs when I am in the strong current and cannot free a hand or leg to swat at it. It makes a painful addition to the plight of continual river crossing. On the other bank, I dry my feet and legs before rolling down my pant legs. I cross the river perhaps twenty times again today, and it seems like a normal and constant phase of movement through this part of the country. It is no more hardship than dealing with fields of tussocks and hummocks, swarms of insects, alder thickets, lack of wood, or any landscape feature that I live with. They are integral parts of this environment I inhabit and move through, and each area has its peculiar features. I adapt to them, concentrate as little as possible on the difficulties that they bring me, and take in the learning that they offer.

I thought that it would be a short hike this morning out of the Kutuk valley to the larger valley of the Alatna River, but it goes on and on for hours. Finally, I break out of the mountains and my whole world changes completely. I am surrounded by open vistas far up and down the Alatna valley. What a huge valley! It is several miles across to the mountains that rise on the west. I feel out in the open, no longer sheltered by the nearness of the Kutuk valley walls and ridges. I can see perhaps twenty miles up and down the valley, which encompasses whole mountains and frames whole groups of clouds. The forests are more open, the trees taller, grander.

The Kutuk loses some of its canyon-cutting energy and slows, becoming a placidly flowing stream with huge, barren gravel bars between stream and forest on one side of the river. Bands of willows and cottonwoods line the main and intermittent channels, and there are patches of a different species of avens with willows above them extending over some of the higher, more stable, undisturbed areas of gravel.

I walk on seemingly forever, anticipating, wanting, dreaming of the Alatna River and the course it will play in my life and travels. Suddenly, while pushing my way through a stand of willows, I see it: "Alatna!" I scream to myself. My heart beats faster, and I run excitedly. I cross the Kutuk for the last time, in leather boots without slowing to roll up my pants. I drop my pack to the gravel and run to riverside. I lie down and run my hand along its clear, smooth, green surface, my eyes along its width. My mind bathes in the satisfaction of having reached this point. The river is deeper than I had expected and, shedding my clothing, I dive in to find it is also much colder than I had expected, colder than lower stretches of the Kutuk. The hills across and up the river are smooth and rolling, covered with spruce and paper birches. It is a stimulating sight, one I have dreamed about for many days.

The elevation here at the river is about a thousand feet, that of the surrounding mountains about four thousand feet, and that of the Arrigetch cluster from six to seven thousand feet. I retrieve my pack, hike a short distance downriver, and find a place to camp in a balsam poplar stand near the river.

I put my fishing pole into action, but again no grayling. I do not know where to fish because the surface looks homogeneous. I am guessing where to toss my fly. But it doesn't matter — the sandbanks provide staples. Fireweed is everywhere and Eskimo potatoes grow in dry sand in large, easily loosened clumps. The rhizomes of these plants are as long and thick as slender carrots. I bake them on a bed of coals at dinnertime. Tonight they taste like sweet potatoes—sugary, soft inside, with a crisp peel. When I have finished eating, I gather more for dessert, as I can find no blueberry bushes on this river gravel.

The whole first part of the trip has seemed like a push to reach this river. I have gotten here, but it has taken me eighteen hard, long days to do it. The big push now is over, and I settle back and see those days behind me. Would I do it again? From Anaktuvuk Pass to here, I must have zigzagged 120 miles — long, tough tundra miles with many rivers, vegetation growth forms, insect populations, raw mountains, and rare feelings. I have gained the understanding of what I have walked through and what it is like to be out here—alone, lonely, unrescuable—in order to experience the Brooks Range. I would do it again.

Rafting starts tomorrow with the initial construction.

PART TWO

Rafting

I have never built a raft and have never floated a river, though I have spent time with rivers, watching them and fishing. In Bettles, Ray Bane (one of the National Park Service men) had told me that the Kobuk natives of years ago used to hike into these mountains in the spring and spend the summer hunting, fishing, and gathering. In the late summer or fall, they would build large rafts and float down the rivers back to their village. The rivers are long, broad, and meandering. Over the years, the natives developed a design for rafts that suited their purposes. An odd number of logs is used, with the longest one in the center. All other logs progressing in jumps are a bit shorter, with the small end of each log at the front of the raft, the big end at the back. It produces a pointed rear end with an expanded width. A cross log is used to lash the raft together at the front and middle, with no crosspieces at the rear. The cross logs are tied to the top of the raft so they will not drag in shallow water. A small rack is built at the rear of the raft for stacking the gathered products of summer (my pack in this case), and a person stands near the front with a long pole to direct the movement of the raft by pushing off objects or the river bottom. The lightness of the front and heaviness of the rear would seemingly cause a friction differential, resulting in the front end going faster than the rear, and thus keeping the front forward in the flow. A square raft would go in any direction, control would be limited, and a rudder necessary.

I unfold my bow saw and take to the forest. Standing dead (but not rotten) trees are the best for my purposes because they are the driest logs and will float the longest. I locate a spruce stand that is closer to the river than other patches of forest and start looking over suitable trees. What a surprise! Almost all the standing dead trees are larger than the up to eight-inch diameter I need. It is incredible that they can grow so large this close to the tree line.

I find a suitable tree about thirty feet tall and saw through it until I almost come through the other end. Then I push on the tree several times to develop a rocking motion; it cracks and topples to the ground. I saw off the branches and the top of the tree and fasten a rope onto it. I start pulling it along the gravel toward the riverside. It is about a hundred yards from the forest to the river and the rope bites a groove in my hand even though I wear leather gloves. It is a long, slow, hard drag, the log being about fifteen feet long and weighing more than I wish to carry. There are several little gullies lined with gravel where I must drag the log down and then up the other side. I lean forward and chug, gritting my teeth where the log catches on a large stone. When I reach a patch of sand near the river, I am able to hold the front part of the log a bit above the sand and skid the log along almost effortlessly.

Up to the riverside I drag it, each step an effort as I concentrate on maneuvering around the rocks and other obstacles that slow progress. I sit by the river for a rest and then head back to the forest to hunt for another log. I am clothed only in leather boots and gloves since days are warm and summery with enough breeze to keep mosquitoes away. Flies are more persistent, however. These huge, biting creatures never land on the front of the chest or the thighs, but always on the back of my legs, buttocks, or neck—always someplace that is difficult to swat. I jump as I walk, dancing to the music I sing and whistle, and I realize that my song has changed. Instead of singing a sad song or questioning why I am here and alone, I sing happy music, lyrics of togetherness and love. I am happy to be here building. Perhaps it is an age-old trait of man to be content when his hands and mind are busy constructing things for himself. Here I build something new, as yet unplanned, and a vessel for my future travel.

I search for another log and find one a bit larger than the first. I take it down, trim it, tie it up, and slowly drag it to the river in the fashion of the first one. I stop for a blueberry break, but find no berries in the woods, so I settle for my lunch biscuits, with honey and peanuts. I try my luck at fishing again, but the swift river shows me no strikes and no fish. I try slow pools, eddies, every place imaginable. I cannot understand why I am unable to find fish in the river.

Log dragging takes all day—solo raft building is slow work. I make it enjoyable, taking my time to choose only the logs I want, taking down only the trees that I need—no crooked, bent, rotten, or still living individuals; only the tall, straight, dead, but not rotten trees. There is an equilibrium with regard to the size of the raft. It must be large enough to float me and my gear down the river, but cannot be too large and heavy to be dragged from sandbars and shallow areas, or even to be pushed off banks and landed each evening or anytime I need to get off the raft.

I ponder a number of questions. How much buoyancy does one log have? How much weight will it float? How much water will the logs absorb sitting in the river in the days to come? Will the logs become saturated with water after being submerged by my weight? How much will the raft weigh when all the pieces are lashed together? Will I be able to budge it from sandbars if it gets caught? These questions trouble me, but as with any other questions, I answer them as best I can and trust my judgment.

I believe that farther downstream from here, the Alatna is a much slower, meandering river, with many sandbars and slow places of shallow water where a raft could get stuck, but only time will tell what I will see. These are leisurely days of construction. The warmth and sandy expanses cause me to lie in the sun. To relax is an emotional experience. Now that I am here at the Alatna, I can rest.

When I see the dew sparkling in the morning's first light, I understand why people give up money to capture a piece of this. Something so pure must be treasure.

The sun climbs over the ridge to the northeast, and with the first rays I can feel the valley warming with the streaming energy of light and heat. Sitting by the river, I eat my ration of granola with powdered milk and raisins. I watch the river's water flow away, constantly replaced by more from the infinite number of valleys, tributaries, gullies, seeps, springs, and snowbanks of this drainage system. I try to think of all the places this water could have come from and I am boggled by the number of named and nameless places and the forms the water has taken before flowing here to compose this moving body. This river's sources and resources are vast and unending, and it is comforting to know that it will not suddenly run out if one spring dries up or when one snowfield gives its last flake. This ribbon of river is the product of diversity. Water has flowed over many types of stones, leaching and carrying many types of minerals and many sediments with intricate histories, all moved again to be deposited elsewhere and begin another history.

I cut two more logs for the raft, drag them over, and put them on the sides. Then I do a final trim to make things as smooth as possible where knobs are left from cut branches. I also cut the lengths of logs to make a symmetrical V-shaped rear end (the front is cut straight across). I make crosspieces from the topped-off sections of the trees, then line it all up and decide how to tie the whole works together. I first put a bowline at the end of the rope and pass the rest through it to make a slip knot. This I place around one end log where the front crosspiece goes, and I cinch it as tightly as possible. I use ground line, which is used in commercial longline fishing for saltwater fish, principally halibut. It is nylon, with a lot of stretch, and has about a thousand-pound test strength, which I hope is strong enough. I wear my goatskin gloves to protect my hands while pulling and knotting. I put my feet on the log, grab the line, and push with my legs and pull with my arms, shoulders, and back as hard and continually as I can.

I continue this for all the logs across the raft, pulling, pushing, wrapping tightly, securing the logs together. I end the line with a series of half hitches to make sure the end will not come loose. Then I lie on the sand to rest my exhausted body. I feel the sun upon my face and watch the clouds drift by. I can feel the river moving near my feet, and I know the great stride I have just taken to move with the river's flow. I had forgotten how incredible human hands are at building. I get up and lash the logs together in the middle of the raft, just as I had in the front. The most important part is to get it all as tight as possible, because the strength of the river could pull apart any flimsily tied raft. This tying and lashing, when finished, gives the whole works a solid feeling as if it were one unit of wood instead of many.

Next I find two long poles, perhaps twice my height and sturdy enough to push the raft in the current without breaking, yet small enough so I can wrap my hands around them and light enough for easy mobility. I also cut four sections of a downed tree and build the small rack on the back of the raft, lashing the rack pieces together and to the raft. It is finished. I pick up the scraps of sawdust and branches and throw them into the river.

Now I stand back and look at the result of my two days' labor, two days' of pleasure, actually. It is a nine-log raft, symmetrically designed with poles and a rack, and tightly lashed—a thing of beauty, created by me to be used by me as a part of my life. I believe it just might float.

The Alatna River valley is a completely different environment from the other valleys I have seen so far. Every morning here is as cool and calm and clear as anyone can imagine. And when I look away toward the south to the great interior of Alaska or north toward the skies over the Arctic plain, I see a mist of cool air that has settled during the brief evening. As the morning heat, which proliferates in these lowlands, causes the air to rise and circulate, some moves into these mountains. Raised by orographic processes, the air heated by the day and the heat of condensation form cumulus clouds. The clouds build into whopper thunderheads that boom and blow until the landscape runs with moisture, the rivers with mud.

The wind picks up in violent gusts. Sand blows along the riverbank and stings my bare legs. I cover my eyes and run toward the trees as a violent downpour begins. I reach camp and huddle under my poncho for the few minutes of downpour, the few crashes of thunder, the few minutes of chill. Then it's over. My bare feet leave prints in the wet sand, the poplars drip until their leaves are dry, and the fresh smell of balsam again fills the air.

As the sun makes its way northward, dipping toward the horizon on its ceaseless circular path, all becomes cool once more. Calm returns and draws the valley into a tiny, closely related unit again. I go back to the raft and see if it needs any further work. It doesn't, and I see it waiting in anticipation of our journey. Now my thoughts run wild with ambition to travel, to try my handmade vehicle.

The day of the trial has come. I pack all my gear and haul it down to the riverside. I munch on breakfast as I lash my pack onto the raft. When all is secured and my belongings packed and ready, I sit on the shore and think. I have some fears about this part of my travels. This is my first rafting experience and I am alone, with no one around to show me how and make sure I start off right. Rivers can never be trusted. They are strong, ceaseless, and capricious. What is visible on the surface does not always indicate what is underneath, what most of the water is doing, and why. I know this can be a great way to travel, but never having floated a river, I am not sure how to make it safe.

I look up the winding valley toward the north and spots of clouds that pattern the sky, and I believe I will learn how to handle this raft very quickly. I plan to travel only a mile or so downriver to where Arrigetch Creek joins the Alatna and then hike up to Arrigetch for a few days of looking at granite pinnacles. I think back to the many days since Anaktuvuk Pass, and I christen my raft *Blueberry*. I wish I had a bottle of blueberry wine to drink (but I would never break a bottle in this valley, not even upon the bow).

I stand up and prepare to be off when I notice a slight complication to my departure. I built the raft on the sand alongside the river, not on logs that I could use to roll it into the water. How could I have been so stupid! I run around to the back and see if I can push it, but it does not budge. The raft is about fourteen feet long and perhaps five feet wide at the widest spot; the weight, I cannot guess. I have constructed a wooden blob that may be immobile. I do not want to untie the lashings, so I move around one side and try to lift it and actually get it a few inches from the ground. Swinging my body toward the river, I shove the raft in that direction, and it moves a few inches. Then I go to the other side and duplicate that motion; again a few inches. It is stressful work, but I keep up the pulling and shoving, with many sweating rests in between, for an hour or so until the front end starts to float. I take a twenty-foot section of ground line and tie it to the longest log at the rear of the raft. I use this as my rein to hold the raft as the current starts to take it downstream. I hold it near shore, then coil the line as I walk toward the raft and try to climb on. I put my foot on one side but it starts to sink, so I go around back where the stern is still on sand and step over my pack. I move forward enough so that the rear rises. I pick up a pole, push against the sand to direct us out into the river, pushing, pushing, gritting my teeth. We are free from sand and floating. Away from the bank we move!

Standing is too hard, as any motion of mine upsets the balance of the floating craft, so I kneel on the logs and use the pole to try to keep the raft pointed forward, but it is difficult. The water is deep, and in places the current is too swift. I plunge the pole into the water, feed it deeper, and then shove to right myself or change the direction of the front end. It doesn't seem to work. I must be doing something wrong, or maybe poling is used only in still water or to push off of large stones. The river seemed so fast from the bank, with water passing by rapidly. But now upon the same waters, it seems much slower. The river is broad and features are big. There is time to see obstructions and react. It is not fast water where I need to manipulate the raft constantly. I start to look around and feel comfortable about being on the river.

I float for an unknown time, a distance of perhaps a mile, until I come to where Arrigetch Creek pours into the Alatna. Poling toward the bank, I look for a place to tie the raft for the several days while I am up the creek. I see a small raised island at the riverside. There are a few spruce trees and a seemingly sheltered cove away from the current. Expansive sand and gravel bars surround it, and it looks as if it would be easy to relocate when I come back from Arrigetch. I steer toward it and grab the reins of *Blueberry*. I put my pole down and for lack of a better way of doing it, jump into the water. It is about crotch deep here and wants to pull me and the raft away, but I manage to land both of us. I tie the rear end line onto a spruce and put another line on the front for safekeeping and also tie it to a tree.

I sort through my gear and take out a few odds and ends that will be unnecessary for the next few days: the saw, bow, and arrows, among other things. I take all my food, though, afraid to leave anything that could provide a meal for a hungry animal.

I hoist my pack for the first time in three days, and it still feels a part of me. Off I walk across the expanse of open, naked gravel into the forest. Bear tracks dot the mud everywhere, and patches of dug-up earth in the forest tell me more bear stories. The forest is open, mossy. Light streams through to the ground, and there are wet areas in lowlands and depressions between small hills.

Blueberries are abundant, and I take time and great pleasure in feasting on these foods that also feel a part of me even though it has been three days since I last tasted them. I even sample the black juicy crowberries, happy to see them, though they are not nearly so sweet as blueberries.

I get to a small, open knoll and look out across the Alatna valley and up to Arrigetch. I dwell for a moment on my most recent experiences. Rafting is different from what I had expected. It is hard to steer and stay in the main current or middle of the river and away from banks, shores, and overhanging trees. I have gone about one mile; one hundred more and I will be a raftsman. Until then, I will just try to keep afloat and intact.

Looking up toward Arrigetch, my eyes are treated to spectacular views. I raise the question of whether or not the mountains are real. I must go touch at least one to satisfy my curiosity. I plan to hike alongside Arrigetch Creek, but soon it shows its rocks, taking on cliffs and grand rapid proportions, forcing me back into the forest. Alder and willow brush is thick, and walking upon the hillsides, I follow the faint netlike patterns of moose paths that are obscured by growth. They zigzag, branching into many routes, but the moose have plowed decent paths, and I follow any route I can. I learn to follow marks, such as broken branches on alders, to note the direction of travel of these biotic bulldozers.

These are long miles with many hills and gullies. Clouds come early this day. They are not the kind of clouds that spit rain, bend the trees with wind, and then go away, but clouds that fill the sky with darkening gray and rain. It is calm and quiet, and starts to drizzle, then rain harder. I crawl under my poncho and wait a while—one hour, two, who knows how long? I nap, awaken, eat, wait. The rain stops, then I walk. The alders get thicker and thicker as if the rain has put endless growth-inducing elements into these soils, and thickets have developed. It turns into a physical challenge to push and bend my way through these dwarf jungles.

The alder leaves are like tiny, precariously perched buckets, each one filled with the rains of this afternoon. Any movement of a branch or leaf causes them to spill. I push branches, and entire shrubs drop their water, and always I am underneath. It is too hard to walk in my loose-fitting poncho so I walk in wool, which soon is damp, then as soaked as it can be.

Mosquitoes come out in hoards and my repellent is soaked and runs all over my face, burning my eyes and lips. Water is everywhere, yet to stop in a brief opening in the forest is immediate pleasure. Berries provide sweetness and alders are green, soaked with shining silver bark. Lichens, swollen with their drinking, abound on the ground and bark. I delight in cooling off during these brief minutes and feeding my stomach and eyes. It is such a needed switch from the bruising work of crashing through alder thickets.

I head toward the creek because I think that walking on its opposite side will be much easier walking than in these alders. But the creek has cut steep cliffs and I dare not attempt to climb them. So I break through brush for the afternoon, always looking for a place to cross the crashing stream. I finally find an outcrop of flat rocks at the riverside and decide to make camp.

I find deadwood and carve it into shavings, some of which are dry. Soon a fire warms my pot of grains and my body. I try to dry my shirt over the fire, and it takes on the incredible stink of wet wool with wet smoke woven into it. I spend several hours holding my clothes by the flames, but it really is just an excuse to warm my body by fire, something I have not yet done on this trip.

This is my first really wet experience. I am soaked from the bottom of my boots to the top of my hat. But my determination to climb into this valley is not dampened, and soon I will be ready to set off again.

I do not set up my tentlike shelter this evening, thinking the rain has ended, as the sky is clearing in patches. I stretch my dry sleeping bag upon a patch of sand alongside the creek, take off my wet clothing, and crawl in. The creek here is a ribbon of rapids and falls. Water rushes over rocks, roaring into the small, deep pool below. This is followed by many loud, rolling rapids. I bathe in the sounds of the creek, living with it these many hours. It is the only noise I hear—no song of a warbler, no jet airplane, no words from a soft-spoken companion. I speak not, and hardly notice the difference between singing and humming, because either mode rings similarly in my mind.

I wake to a dry world. Clouds are moving across the sky, but I believe they will clear, and my life can continue the same as it has. I find a riffle where I can cross the creek. Here the river is moving very swiftly, but the water is not so deep as it is in other parts of the creek. There are some large boulders in the riffle, causing the water to boil and form eddies on the downstream side.

I put on my tennis shoes, roll my pants above my knees, and grab a tight hold on a newly cut pole. I start across the creek slowly; I have not crossed anything on this trip that moves with such vigor. The water is colder than the water of the Kutuk and I guess that this water has not traveled very far from its source, the Arrigetch glaciers. My feet are numb in just a few steps. I move farther into deeper water. Where it gets over my knees, I hold the pole on my downstream side, using it to balance my weight as I continuously fight being pushed downstream by the powerful creek. The valley is steep here, and the water bubbles and rushes past with great velocity. I cannot believe that I am trying to cross this thing. I step behind one of the boulders in the stream, but the water is much deeper, and I am mid-thigh deep, with water splashing, forced even higher up my legs. I am not even halfway across the creek. I step into a small chute where the water rushes between two boulders, and my legs are almost immediately swept out from under me. I am quick with my pole, however, and brace myself. I take two more quick, short steps to a calm, swirling, deep eddy behind another boulder. I work across the creek like this. With reddened, cold legs, I waddle through the shallow water at the river's edge and weakly step up onto the bank. I roll over on my back, unstrap my pack, and roll away from it. I hold my legs up in the air, shake the water from them, and let the gentle breeze dry me. Then I roll down my wet pants and let them dry out, too.

This side of the creek, facing north, is much more open and

definitely is the more favorable side for walking. There are fewer patches of dense alders, few ravines, and lots of open stands of spruce, along with heather, Labrador tea, bearberries, Eskimo potatoes, fireweed, blueberries, and a great array of mosses and lichens.

I come upon a widening in the valley bottom, cross a side channel of the main creek, and walk out onto a small island. It is covered with mountain avens, some willow patches, and a small flat level spot where I stop, drop my pack, and decide to go no farther. I want to camp where the two forks of Arrigetch Creek join, but where I stop is not far downstream. Besides, I am tired and can walk a lot faster and smoother without a pack.

I set up my shelter in this little area where I have a view up both forks. In the center of the valley where the two creeks join is the closest mountain, a mammoth cone rising from the valley and ending in two peaks, each standing as a sentry for the valleys. I leave my pack here and hike up onto a bench to the south to get a closer view of the peaks in that direction. They seem to be the backbone of the range, and are characterized by countless small and many large pinnacles. Their most distinguishing feature is the absolute smoothness of their skins.

I hike back down the short distance to the roaring creek and realize that this valley bottom is an amazingly noisy place due to the rushing, moving force of the creek. On top of the bench the air was almost silent; I heard only branches moving in the wind and the call of an occasional bird. The more westerly drainage is covered with clouds, but the maps describe it as the home of the highest peak in the area. It surely must be a giant to be larger than those that I can see from here.

I feel so independent now. I can go or be anywhere I want to. I have the few essentials I need, and the few other things I need or want I can derive from the land. It is a grand feeling to be able to come up here for a few days on a whim. I had heard that this is a very popular spot for visitors because of the grandiose mountains, but I feel that I am all alone.

I unpack my sleeping bag, put it into my shelter, and get out a pot and the fixings for dinner. I collect a few old scraps of willow branches, start a small fire between two rocks, and get my grains boiling. Then I go to the forest to try to find some blueberries, but I do not find a single blue fruit. I am discouraged because I had thought that this valley had everything, but without blueberries, I am missing a vital aspect of Alaska goodness. I guess that the summer here at three thousand feet is just too cold for the production of many berries in an average year.

I come back to camp and while writing in my journal, I suddenly hear something moving through the brush. I sit still, thinking perhaps it is a moose. Then, all of a sudden, I hear the word, "Hi," and turning around, I see a two-legged creature with leather boots and glasses in front of his eyes. My eyes open wide, and I almost do not know what to do. I had not really wanted to see people, but now that I am face to face with a young man of about my age, I am excited. I have not seen people for twenty-two days. "Are you up here alone?" he asks.

"Holy mackerel," I say. "So there are still humans in the world. Yeah, I'm up here alone. Haven't talked to anyone in three weeks."

"Oh, you must be Cooper," he says. I am shocked that he would know me by name.

He is David Schmitz, a guide for an outfit in Bettles. He had heard about me in the grocery store. The fellow he works for also owns a grocery store. He is up here with a woman from Ohio, or some such place, who has hired him to take her into the wilderness to see the granite spires of Arrigetch.

We are joined by the woman, and I started talking and realize that I haven't really talked since the last time I saw people back in Anaktuvuk Pass and Bettles many weeks ago. It is a funny feeling to catch myself suddenly doing something that is so natural, and realize that a lot of natural life processes are done only in the company of other people. And now I am talking as if I have not ever talked and have saved up all my words. It is an exhilarating experience that everyone takes for granted. I have never realized how satisfying exchanging ideas with other people can be. I think of my life anywhere else, and almost always there have been daily interactions with people. Every one of those interactions could have been just as special as this one, if I only had realized it.

I tell of the logistics of my trip so far, and they really cannot understand what the hiking is like. Maybe nobody else will be able to either. That's kind of scary to me, because I want so much to share these days with other people. David wonders how I could have been living on the marginal food rations that I have had. What kind of meat have I been eating? I tell him I have caught grayling whenever I could, but the Kutuk and Alatna have spared me no fish, and so I have not had meat in a long time. I wonder whether I look hungry or skinny; I think the concern about my diet is pretty funny and I tell them about all the wild roots and assorted other goodies. He says he has heard about eating Richardson's saxifrage leaves. This is Alaska *Boykinia*, and the leaves are bitter and would make anyone a pessimist about the consumption of wild plant matter on a regular basis, though in an emergency, almost anything can be tolerated for awhile. I smile about this, too, because I know that my understanding of the plants around here has provided me with a great wealth of variety and freshness in my skimpy diet. I tell them about Eskimo potatoes, fireweed, bistorts, and all the other delights of this natural world, but they cannot imagine how good these things can be.

They look at my pot of cooking rice and go back to their camp for some freeze-dried dinner of their own. I eat my meal alone and remember the days when I had wished I had someone with whom I could talk and share. It really feels like a different valley now, knowing that other people are here. My journey does not feel as if it is such a great adventure and exploration anymore. I feel good to be here, and the mountains have not lost any of their majestic qualities, but I feel as if I am on an island of humanity in a sea of wilderness. I guess the wilderness is seasonally colonized by groups of humans, and, like everywhere else, there will be only more and larger "human islands" as time goes on.

I hike back up the bench to the south and get a good look at some of the mountains. Part of the walk up is through open meadows covered with mountain avens, the seed heads of which are a cluster of plumes. At the end of each plume is a seed, which is caught and dispersed by the wind. There are also isolated spruce trees, as this area is right at the limit of trees growing in this valley. The trees are tall and healthy and are unlike the tree-limit spruce I am used to in the Rocky Mountains. In the Rockies, the trees are dwarfed and gnarled by the wind, and clearly show the effects of their environment. Here the trees are well formed and possibly are not at the limit of tree growth. They may merely be at their farthest step thus far in a march up the valley, colonizing areas that could not support trees during the last glaciation.

In open meadows, alders are growing as individuals, attaining great height and tremendous proportions. In the evening light, the leaves take on a yellow glow and the landscape is a patchwork of many shades of green. I hike up to a small outcrop of rock and sit still. From here with my binoculars, I scan the sides of the smooth, exposed granite, polished by the same glaciers that have advanced from the shaded corners of the high basins and chased the trees from this valley several times in the past hundred thousand years. The ridge of mountains to the south is magnificent. On the left are a row of three peaks, all two to three thousand vertical feet, and all symmetrical and smoothly proportioned. To their right is a jagged ridge. One peak on this ridge looks like a thumb, one an eagle's head, one a column. Then there is another high section with three more peaks clustered together.

The sun casts pink impressions upon the stone and the whole valley becomes rosy and gently textured. The peaks seem so far away, and at the same instant, so close that I could reach out and touch them. My heart finds a place for this sight and tucks it safely away forever.

JULY 28

A hard, hard rain has fallen all night. And now looking out of my shelter, I can see that it is drizzling, and the clouds are hanging in the valley, so that all I can see are the bottoms of ridges. On this trip, I have not lazily spent one morning in the sack, as there has always been too much to do. Now as I listen to the rain on my roof, it is a delight to lie here and be lazy, sleeping some extra hours and using the rain as an excuse for relaxing, even though there is no reason to make excuses and no one to tell them to.

I have been carrying the first book of Tolkien's *Lord of the Rings* trilogy for just such an occasion. It is entertaining, but reading books almost seems like an escape, a way to pass the hours and dreary minutes when there is not enough to experience in this, my own world. I rebel for an instant and put the book down, but realize that I cannot go out into the soggy, chilling world and stay warm, dry, and content for very long. Here I have an opportunity to experience the products of another mind. I know the rain will clear any minute, and I will be able to go out and explore the area.

I read, sleep, read, sleep, roll around, test every position I can dream up, and still run out of possibilities for comfort. Six or eight extra hours of this is bad for the body, and I am developing aches in every conceivable place. The highest spot in my tent is not quite high enough for sitting upright. I am really starting to experience something new for me this summer—the inconvenience of doing or being whatever the weather will allow. It rains, and I must do what I can to stay dry and warm, to maintain health in this frail body that my life occupies. I cannot go out and dance about in the cold rain. I cannot go out and crawl among the tundra plants and see their swollen forms and the drops gathered by their leaves. Instead I am restricted to this tiny shelter and to my own mind for entertainment and satisfaction during these hours.

I think of my life here in these mountains these past weeks, and I see that it really has been the experience I have wanted. I am here to see more than just mountains—I also want to see myself and be without most of the modern comforts. I forced myself to walk away from civilization into a place where I cannot take the basics for granted. A healthy body is the only means by which my mind can survive here. I must take care of myself, and it takes a lot more time than I had imagined. There are no fossil fuels to speed along a hot dinner on the stove or motor me across the valley, no warm shelter in which I can move freely. Here, I must first of all keep warm, which is not easy. The temperature must be in the forties, the winds are becoming very strong, and, of course, there is the rain and the wet, humid, sticking cold. I stay inside my sleeping bag and stay warm, eating a cold breakfast and cold lunch fixed the night before and drinking the water that drips from the tent into my water bottle. Simple solutions are the answer for everything here, and they are not the same solutions relied upon in civilization or in any permanent outpost of human habitation. The entire real world is the nature of life in the Brooks Range, and I have been living naturally.

My friend comes over carrying an aluminum dish of warm leftover dinner. I am not sure whether it is left over because they are full or because they feel sorry for me. No matter. It is a nice gesture, and I appreciate the warm food. There is even a piece of meat in it, he tells me, and smiles warmly, and I am amazed that freeze-dried Colorado beef can be prepared to enjoy in the remote mountains of the world. The meal provides me with a chance to compare freeze-dried food, which is what many modern outdoor people feed themselves, with my basic staples of grains. The flavors are abundant, and though I do not know the name of the product, I wonder whether I could live longer on the basics that I have had than on these packaged meals.

We exchange a few words, but it is raining, and soon I am alone again. The wind billows my shelter as it enters one end and exits out the other. There are no physical comforts now, but knowing that I am experiencing this environment exactly the way it is relieves the pains in my body and extinguishes the boredom in my mind. I lie quietly on my back, my head sticking out of my sleeping bag, listening to the rain and the beat of my heart.

Blueberry (*Vaccinium uliginosum*)

Rain again, nonstop. I lie on my back and try to sleep through the hours of chill and cloudy drizzle. I curl to one side, then to the other. There are only so many sides that I can choose, and none of them can hold my interest for very long. The pain in my lower back becomes too much and I get out of my bag, put on all my clothing, and walk around for awhile. But the wind is up and the rain is upon my wool clothing, so I am forced back to the shelter. I wonder whether it is raining in all the valleys of the Brooks Range. The Arrigetch Peaks are much higher than most of the surrounding ridges and summits, and I wonder whether that has something to do with this continuous rain.

I think back to the past three weeks of this trip and the fine weather I have had. I have been active every day until now, and surely the weather has permitted my movement across the mountain range. Now, lying here, I wonder what I would have done if the weather had been like this the whole time. How far would I have made it, and would I have learned to cope with the wet weather and hiked right through it? It is bad enough being in the tussocks and hummocks when they are dry. If they had been soaked, I would have been miserable. The tiny fragments of wood that I have used for fires would surely have been soaked right through, so fire would have been difficult to make. What a real problem that could have been.

The winds are not so strong as they were yesterday, and I get wise and sit under a big spruce tree on the hillside to cook myself a hot dinner. I gather branches of dead alder to avoid breaking branches off the spruce trees, as other visitors have done. It is all wet, but I peel off the bark, exposing the wood, and split some of it lengthwise to get a fire burning. I bring three rocks up from the river to hold my pot as I cook. This is the smokiest campfire I have ever seen. Every piece of wood is wet, and the smoldering heat releases sappy moisture, clouding my little spot and burning my tender eyes. It is hot though; I can get my water boiling and grains cooking.

I lean back against a tree and try to read as the fire cooks. The tree is a perfect shelter, and the light rain does not touch me, but the wind is much stronger here on the hillside. I stand up, jumping to generate heat, but I cannot warm up. I sit back down and curl into a nook of the tree and try to hide from the wind. It doesn't work. I curl around my fire and steep in the smoke and heat that rise from the wood, but by the time the effect of the fire has come beyond the pot, it is mostly smoke and not much heat. I could make a huge blaze with the available dead wood, but this valley is already touched by humans, and I would rather be cold now, and the whole time I am here, than to use this finite wood supply to heat my body.

When the grain is cooked, I add several spoonfuls of margarine to increase my caloric intake. I quickly slurp it all down so I can return to my shelter to warm my outer body while my inner organs have warm food to work with. I push the ashes around a bit, then leave them for the ubiquitous rain to cool and wash away.

I see my friends again, and they tell me that it is Thursday. I had been wondering, because the mail plane in Allakaket comes in only twice a week on specific days. I need to know what day it is when I reach that point so that I do not have to wait in the village for several days. Because I may not see any other people for the remainder of the trip, I store this bit of information in my journal.

How funny it is to think about the day of the week. It really doesn't matter out here what day it is because I do what I have to do every day. I do not do anything special on Friday night, or on Sunday. Only the nature of the area is different every day, and to that I respond. Seasonal changes would result in definite behavioral changes, but I do not have to cope with that. I know that somewhere out there in the cities everyone knows it is Thursday and is going about Thursday business. But for me it is simply today.

July 30

After a night with the clouds hanging at my nose, I awake to see blue sky. I jump and yell and smile at the bright sunshine. As I eat a quick breakfast of the usual granola, I sit and look up at the peaks, these giants of the rock world, then I look down toward the Alatna River. That valley is socked in, and the mountains farther to the east are covered with clouds. As I finish my breakfast, I lose my smile. I see the clouds coming up the valley and soon engulfing the whole area — no more sun, no more view of the peaks or of anything else; only clouds and the bits of vegetation that lie at my feet. My excitement and inspiration drain out of me as the moisture in these clouds begins to drain out onto the surfaces of the valley. I crawl back into my shelter, weary from the effects of disappointment.

I read as the rain drips and drips. I wish I had not eaten my breakfast so fast, because lying in the tent with only a book and a pen, I would love to have enough to eat to keep at least my hunger satisfied. When I eat my half cup of granola bit by bit and chew each bit to the maximum extent, it seems like a real meal and I can go a few hours without wanting more chewing. But today, I gobbled the mass down in a few minutes. Neither the gap in my belly nor in my mind is full, and I now am in great need of another breakfast.

Luckily for me, my friends had given me some of their extra supplies when they had left this morning. They were hiking to the Alatna River to meet a plane that would take them to town, so they did not need them. I could not thank them enough, but they knew how much I appreciated the extra things after so many days and weeks of the same basic foods. They gave me a little package of trail snacks made up of nuts, dried fruit, and sweetened grains, and a small package of mission figs. I had run out of dried fruit, except for raisins, more than a week ago. I look at them all eagerly, then tear the plastic of the trail snacks and pour out a small handful. I put down my book and concentrate on each morsel of this treat. As I put one piece into my mouth, I am already concentrating on which piece I shall choose next. It is such a great diversion from the words and from my supine position while the rain pitters on the earth. I tell myself that I will just nibble on this little pile that rests in my palm, but when that amount is beginning to wane, I cannot help dipping into the package to replenish the pile. I cannot stop myself, and do not try very hard. This is exactly what I need on a rainy day—something to keep my hand, mouth, and stomach busy.

It is not long before I crumple up the empty trail snacks package. Where did all of it go? I had not intended to eat it all. I settle back down to read some more, satisfied, but it is not very long before I remember the figs. Funny, at the same instant, I remember David Schmitz's words as he gave me these gifts. "If you spread these out, they should last you a long time." I get a little embarrassed thinking of my lack of self-control, but I have exercised continual control in all kinds of situations in these mountains, so I do not worry that I am disregarding good advice by not spreading the treats out for a week or so. The fate of the bag of mission figs is the same as that of the trail snacks. One by one, I rid myself of the need to munch, and soon all the figs are eaten. The bag is empty, and I laugh that at least I have gotten it out of my system.

I finish the first book of Tolkien's trilogy and, as I end it, the rain ceases. I peer up toward the clouds, which are moving west to east at a very fast pace. There are patches of blue tucked in among the grays of the clouds, and the valley begins to open up. I dress quickly and get ready to go see some of Arrigetch. There is no rain, but the wind is steady and the feeling of being exposed to the elements that formed these raw mountains creeps up inside of me. It is a feeling known from the most severe parts of any range, areas above which no native life lives and rock, snow, ice, and wind take over.

I had been told of some lakes that sit way up one valley and I head there. I hike up the riverside from camp and it is overgrown with dense alders, making me bend and twist and break my way upstream. A beautiful waterfall plunges over a bedrock bench here, and I sit and listen to its roar for many minutes. Up and over I climb, continuing upstream. The stream is a maze of boulders, almost as many boulders in the stream as on the land. I try walking on these boulders and find it easier going than the streamside. I cross to the other side of the river and head out across the tundra. There are no trees up this far, and the vegetation is very low. Mats of reindeer lichens abundantly cover the ground. Piles of rocks and talus are completely encrusted with big platelike rock-tripe lichens. The environment is marginal for growth because of the shortness of the growing season and cool temperatures, but every undisturbed inch of this land is covered with some life-form. The valley is magnificent in its diversity. Looking back toward the Alatna River, the area looks dry and unspectacular with no single feature to cause attraction. But then, looking south to the backbone of the array of the Arrigetch Peaks, I am overwhelmed by their abrupt vertical relief and smooth character. I continue upstream and follow a fork that heads up a steep valley to the west. I climb higher and higher along the thin creek and its rock sides, over fields of mountain avens and steep, slippery, lichen-covered talus.

Higher I go, and the mountain on the right comes closer and closer and the valley narrows. There are huge talus slopes radiating from the bases of all the peaks. These are the work of countless years of freeze-thaw cycles that pried slabs from the parent stone and toppled them into these streams of debris where the lichens now find a home. I can see cliffs on the right as the ridge there plunges almost vertically to the gound at a point where I presume the first lake is. I come through the low point in the valley, just above a small plunging series of falls, and find a lake.

I stand still for a moment, surveying the rim of this basin. I feel as if I have discovered some unknown treasure, walked into some paradise of nature, never before observed. I can see two lakes—small, deep and as dark blue and pristine as can be imagined. There are a few rocks at the edges that stand out of the water, but the water becomes deep so fast that there are almost no shallow areas. Along the north and west sides of this first lake, the vertical wall rises from its scattered talus into a long ridge that runs back to the second. It is hundreds of feet high, made of plate after plate of overlapping granite spread out like a hand of cards. The valley continues up beyond the second lake, and I can see a small stream descending from where more lakes are located.

From the far side of the first lake, I look back across the water. There is one small mountain, and then the backbone of Arrigetch rises in the distance—raw granite peaks, standing in a string, each set apart and connected to the rest. I see the peaks, and I see their reflection in the calm, still water of the lake. It is the eeriest feeling I can remember, as if I were not in this world at all, but in some fairyland of calmness and picture-book mountains. And all the while, the fierce clouds roll overhead, frightening and threatening, but unable to touch me or my visions. Wind slides across the lake surface, ruffling its smooth character. Reflections of my panorama become slightly smeared as in a pastel-shaded watercolor by Monet. The sharp images of mountains, which the wind cannot bend, and their reflections are spread end to end before me.

What can I feel, what should I feel among the finest mountains in the world? They are only rock, yet they will live on and on, as countless Eskimo and mountain men have seen throughout the ages, and as thousands of white men soon will see. These mountains provide inspiration because their majestic qualities draw out man's majestic qualities and feelings. I could write forever about this moment and this feeling. But do these mountains draw from me things that before lay only beneath the surface of my skin? Why have I come here, anyway? Do these mountains bring me sorrow, as I know that all other mountains are lesser and I will always have to compare other sights, other feelings, with this moment? But they are only rock, cold slabs, thrust up from the bowels of the earth by some unthinkable forces of nature and honed to their present form by other forces that continuously change the world.

Suddenly, I am alone again. The wind blows down the valley and a shiver runs up my spine. The clouds close in. Ripples and waves move across the lake, and my mirror image of paradise is distorted and swallowed up by the depthless emerald arms of the lake. The peaks turn gray and less grand, their tops absorbed and removed by the rushing clouds. Why do I come here to find inspiration from rock? Why haven't I chosen to find inspiration from people, who might also find inspiration in me? I am here loving rock, and now I feel the unloved feeling these rocks emit. They are cold and impersonal. People should worship the people they live with, for they are the only things on earth they can know, love, trust, and live and die with.

I make my way back around the edge of the lake. The vegetation is remarkably lush, probably due to the great amount of humidity in the basin. Lichens and mosses grow in huge clumps and mats, and heaths mingle among the rocks and build hummocks of their own. I descend the valley and stop to dig some roots on the side of a warm, well-drained slope that overlooks the river. The soil is rocky. Although I try to pry the rocks out of the way, I do not have much luck. I gather only a few potatoes for my pot, but there is an abundance of bistort and sorrel leaves. I nibble on a few willow leaves and find them quite palatable, too.

I return to my flimsy shelter on the small island between two braids of the river. I find a few willow and alder twigs and start a small fire in a gravelly gap between two larger boulders. There is heat to warm my pot, but none left over to warm me—another warm meal for a cold body.

It is a silent night, with occasional sweeps of wind that run down the neck of my sleeping bag. I sleep soundly, unaware of changes taking place in the atmosphere above my head, then wake to a sunny world. Opening my eyes for the first time, I quickly loosen the top of my bag, zip it down, and crawl out to feel the sun on my skin. The air is not warm, but there are no clouds. Everything sparkles, still wet from the past day's rain. It seems like forever since I have seen the sun, and I point my face toward it to feel this new warmth.

All the peaks are fully exposed. Water runs down their granite faces in thin ribbons, giving the stone a striped effect. The area is quite appealing now that all its facets can be seen, but not so dramatic as when partially hidden in cloud. I munch on breakfast and decide to take a short hike up the north valley before heading down to the Alatna River. I hike up Arrigetch Creek, crossing the south fork and following the north fork. I walk along the large flood plain, through patches of willows and alders and open meadows of mountain avens, grasses, sedges, and herbs. I cross the north fork in a few leaping bounds between large rocks and run out onto the broad, open slopes that spread out at the base of the steep valley walls. Everything in the meadows and the shrubs at streamside are green. Mats of moss campion are spread upon the land with the occasional white blossom of an anemone. Ripening seeds of all plants rest on stalks. Huge alluvial fans spread out upon the lower slopes of this valley, and I can see great fields and ribbons of talus radiating from peaks, down the slopes. There are intricate patterns of fragmented rock, strips of vegetation, and bedrock outcrops that produce mosaics upon the landscape.

I hike only a little way up the valley. I can see to its end, and it is quite a good way farther. In the center of the valley is the sliverlike peak that I recall seeing in photographs of this valley. I sit for awhile along the stream where it cuts a little canyon through limestone. The ground is moist and shaded here, with the broad herbaceous leaves of Alaska *Boykinia* spread out everywhere. Abundant mosses and tiny ferns grow upon the dripping limestone cliffs. I listen to the churn of water that digs deeper into the bedrock each second. This valley is paradise today, with the sun to warm the air and make sight-seeing a pleasure. But I have been here long enough. I came to see these peaks, and though I have seen them only a little, I have felt their presence. Now that the weather has finally cleared up and summer has returned, I want to head down the valley to the Alatna and find my raft.

Back at camp it takes only a short while to gather the few things that I have brought. I take one last look at the gallery of granite, then start down. I am into alder immediately and find many thin, capricious trails wrought by the feet of caribou and human visitors. I can follow these trails for short distances and must continuously look for scars where before I was constantly looking at virgin country for a way to pass by. It is quite a different concept in walking. The still summery day continues, with hardly a wisp of wind. Because of the warmth, I am glad that I am descending this valley instead of ascending it. It is a long, long walk toward the river, and I turn and stare with awe at the peaks that gradually drop farther and farther away.

The walk is quite enjoyable as I soon find blueberries, exhibiting their season's produce. I feast all day, making up for all the days when I lay at Arrigetch, dreaming of them. Looking over to the north side of the creek I hiked up before, I can see why I had so much difficulty. It is densely vegetated, with many gullies and ravines, and crowded with thickets of alder that were horrible to get through. This side is open forest with some wet sedge meadows and fields of talus crusted over by brittle lichens. Occasional springs erupt from the bedrock, surrounded by an entourage of mosses and wet-loving plants. I cross four streams. Each one is a plunging, delightfully refreshing environment with lush vegetation, sparkling water, and fall after splashing fall.

I can see only a short distance up these streams. My imagination flies off to remote basins and lingering patches of winter's snow where these tumbling waters originated. I take a special fancy to each stream and wish I had a whole week to walk the length of each one's course, for I know how remote and unexplored these small tributary valleys are. In these mountains, even major drainages are seen only occasionally by foot travelers. The small tributaries are almost never visited.

At the mouth of the Arrigetch valley, where it joins the open expanse of the Alatna valley, is a series of small, flat-topped hills. They are perfectly dry, with a sparse covering of crowberries, lingonberries, and lichens. Tall spruce trees frame the grand view back to the open extended fingers of the Arrigetch Peaks, and the series of valleys comprising the area. Five hundred feet below me, I can hear the faint rumble of Arrigetch meltwaters as they move toward the sea. To the east, in a north-south line, opens the huge Alatna valley. I can see far upstream past the Unakserak River and downstream past the Pingaluk River, both major tributaries of the Alatna. It is a wonderful view of the country that I have called home this past week.

I start down from the dry hills toward a spot on the river where I believe the raft is. These slopes are a maze of hummocks upon which bog birches grow, sending branches along the ground surface to tangle with branches of other birches. It seems as if little wires are stretched out across the hummocks and I am continually catching a foot on these invisible traps and falling to the ground. It is always hard to stand back up because of my pack. Fortunately, it is a downhill stretch and I can take long strides, trying to stay in the low spots between hummocks. But, of course, there are tussocks to trip me and slow my walking to a place-one-step-then-the-other-step pace.

On this slope, several small outcrops of bedrock and deposits of glacial till rise up just above the sea of hummocks. I feel as if I am on an island when I ascend one. There are usually a few birch trees with peeling white bark for me to lean back upon, and pendulous, deciduous leaves to provide shade. The outcrops form small hills that have an abundance of crowberries growing upon them, and the berries are in their prime of juiciness. They are so abundant on the small creeping shrubs that I can grab a branch, flatten my index finger and thumb together (parallel to each other), and, keeping my palm open, move my hand down the branch and have all the berries fall into my palm. I then pop the handful of berries into my mouth and get a succulent mouthful of juice in just a few seconds.

With patient, individual steps, I eventually return to the flood plain forests, which are composed of white spruce in the well-drained areas and black spruce in the boggy areas. With the white spruce are willows, alders, and other shrubs forming a crisscross mass of branches. With the black spruce are tussocks, but no nasty shrubs. What a choice. In some places, the forest is rather open (with no shrubs), and walking is simple. In places like this, Eskimo potatoes grow abundantly, and large areas have been uprooted by bears looking for the rhizomes of this plant. I know how difficult it is to dig in these soils, yet it looks as if a bulldozer has come through the area, setting its blade to work here and there. The strength of these animals is hard to believe. Now that I am aware that bears are around, I do not feel safe, as my only protection is a tree I could climb in an emergency. I walk slowly, looking around me all the time for movement. It is funny to be scared again. I had forgotten what it is like.

I reach the river in a short while after waltzing through the luxuriant, boreal forest. I look upstream and downstream to orient myself and head to the north, toward a small island in the river. Sure enough, *Blueberry* is waiting for me. The ropes are still tied as I had left them, but my leather gloves are gone. I cannot guess whether the river was high enough at one point during the rains to sweep them away or whether some animal interested in their salt content made off with them. I am glad I did not leave my food for the raft trip here.

I hike across the gravel bar back to the forest and set up camp. Evening comes slowly, quietly in the valley. I leave my fire and bubbling grains to themselves and walk the few feet to the riverbank. I hang my legs over the bank and gaze at some distant mountains far to the north. Yellows and maroons are spread out across the water of the river, and all the vegetation takes on golden hues and silhouettes. The limestone cliffs near the Pingaluk River are dramatically etched in shades of gray and brown. Above my head, the air is calm, relaxed, and suspended and I wait for evening to lower it upon me as my blanket for sleep.

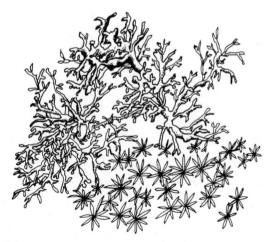

Moss and lichens

August 1

The sun is up over the mountains to the east, and light filters through the tall spruce trees. I can see the water—clear, deep, and strong—and the sound of drops rubbing upon the bank and against each other fills my ears. I look at the river knowing that I will live with it for an unknown period of time as I flow with it to Allakaket. It is hard for me to understand just how many miles I must go or how many hours it will take. Though I can see it on the map, the country between here and my destination is unimaginable. I have no idea what my life will be like, how I will spend my hours, or how much energy this rafting will require—questions, always questions, with answers coming as needed. One feeling this country creates is that of self-sufficiency. When I need something, I make it or build it or gather it myself. It is a great experience knowing that I can make my life from this world I have chosen.

I crawl from my sleeping bag into the calm air of a glorious day. There is a light dew on the blueberry bushes and other leaves. I gather some naturally washed fruit and pack all my gear. I sit in the forest for a moment, feeling the firm tissues of the earth, the tall cylinders of wood, the green of plant life. I think of the land and how many days I will spend on water—a ribbon of water flowing between two land masses, two continents. Two shores I will have; two lives I will lead, life on land and life on the river. The forest is filled with the smells of fallen leaves and ripe fruit. Insects hum. Piles of old logs are rotting. I know these forests; I have lived closely with them. But now I choose to go to the river and start south on my raft, leaving behind my all-day hikes across the land surface.

I lash my gear onto the rack at the back of the raft and put on tennis shoes, then loosen the lines and hop on. Poling out into the current is easy, and I flow smoothly, silently, effortlessly away. I look back to the spot from which I launched and watch it sink farther and farther away. The movement of the raft is almost imperceptible. The flow of water is so continuous, so superficially the same. The only clue to my progress comes as I watch the trees on the bank and compare them with the mountains in the distance. It is my perspective, and I again love the soundless way I am washed downstream.

As I stand on the raft, I find it is too tipsy for much movement, so I pole over to the riverside and beach the raft. I find a recently fallen spruce and cut four small sections from the top of the tree. I lay two sections across the raft logs just in front of my rack, then lay the other two sections across the top of these and tie it all together to make a seat. My feet get too tired standing up, and I may as well sit back and enjoy the country.

Rafting is still something strange and new to me. I do not respond automatically and so act cautiously. I find that I can paddle with my pole, using it as if it were a kayak paddle, to change the direction of the front end of the raft. It is really handy and helps me keep the front into the current.

The river is a winding waterway, and I float through meander after meander. The water moves swiftly in the bends, forcing the current and the raft against the bank. The continuous eroding of the bank causes mature trees to fall into the river. Some of them are still rooted in the bank and lie across the river, collecting other debris. They sweep the water and are called "sweepers." I try with all my newfound skill, muscle, and energy to paddle away from them. They scare me at first, but I avoid them all and soon do not worry about them.

Coming around one bend I see a huge jam of logs, but I relax and wait to see what the current will do. I think it will take me away from the logs, but instead it heads me right toward them. I paddle with all my strength, but my efforts are futile. As in a bad dream, the raft goes on top of a whole series of logs in an instant, with one log trying to go over the top of the raft. The raft stops suddenly, jarringly. Now I feel the real strength of the river. Like a tidal wave that won't stop, the force of the river is full upon this flat span of logs that has ceased to move. The weight and force of water pull and push the raft down. I stand up and the water is instantaneously knee-deep. My seat floats away, then I see my map case floating away. I dive into the water, rescue my maps, and swim back to the raft. Responses here are innate; there is no time to learn what to do, no moments to think. The raft is sinking deeper, thigh-deep at the rear. I run to the front and lift up on the log that is causing this dangerous situation. The force of the river pushes the raft along, and I work the log over the top. Then it catches on my rack and my pack frame. All the force of the river is on my raft, which is held to this log by my pack. Everything is underwater. I am responding with strength I did not know I had. I cannot believe what is happening. I know that I am going to lose my pack, all my gear, the whole raft. I say to myself, "It's over. It's all over. Maybe I'll die of exposure in the hours to come."

I grab my pack frame with my left hand and, cradling the log under my right arm, I lift the log. I hold onto the pack for dear life. I am in the balance, grasping for the present and future and fighting the environment. The log comes free, drags over the top of my pack, and I push it past the back. The raft is free. I am hip-deep in water, but the raft immediately starts to rise. I move to the middle of it, and it starts moving away from the sweeper that nearly has eaten the raft and me alive.

I cannot believe what has just happened. I am fine one minute, then almost lose the whole works, then simply float away. I am stunned. I stare blankly as the raft moves along just as it had before the jam. I realize that I am crying, and I am sure that it must be because I am happy to have survived without losing something or everything. My hands start to shake, the fear of the incident and its real impact just beginning to surface. My body is stiff, my muscles rigid, like panel boards set upon my body.

I want to get off the river now to relax, let the fears subside, and allow my muscles and mind to become calm again. But I know that I must regain my confidence here on the river. I must learn to respect my abilities again. If I get off the river, I will definitely be afraid to get back on it. So I stay on, and the raft flows calmly away as the crisis fades farther and farther behind me. I listen to my heartbeat, listen to the gurgle of a tiny tributary that spills over the bank and splashes into the river. I watch the spruce trees on the bank pass by and follow the line of mountains against the sky. My mind is at once adapted to the pace of the moving water, to the passing of miles, of hills, of mountains, and it all soothes me.

I look down at the logs I stand on and mull over the natural properties that let them float, that let them, lashed together, become my mode of transportation through the waterway scenes of the Alatna valley. All scrapes of our mishap are seemingly gone, the logs washed clean. The flow of the river lends no hints, but the visions remain in the back of my mind, the bad dream that I cannot forget.

The river meanders in huge loops, as if a length of string once was tossed to the valley, and the bent, confused line became the waterway. I must travel much more than a mile to get a mile down the valley. Some loops go straight across the valley, some even go backward. I have only tastes of heading straight south. The valley must be two miles wide here, with high mountains on both sides. A deep canyon cuts its way out of the mountains to the west, and near the mouth of the Pingaluk River stands a great cliff, bare and showing the naked character of the rock that composes these mountains.

I get off the river to build another seat and collect blue-berries. I notice that my tennis shoes are nowhere to be found. They probably floated off when the raft was sinking. Luckily my boots were tied to my pack, or I would have lost them, too. Back on the river, the sun beats down, shining with mirrored brightness off the smooth Alatna. My skin is hot, and I move the bill of my cap at every different bend of the river to shade my face. I do not need mosquito dope here. On the river there are few troublesome insects, except for big biting flies that buzz by and, discovering me, return. Their loud noise breaks the otherwise silent atmosphere, but the feeling of floating and the gentle breeze that stirs the spruce trees continue.

I look back up the river to where the Kutuk enters the Alatna valley. Already it looks far, far away, and gives me the feeling that I am making great strides of distance. But the current is slow, creeping slow, and only time seems to take me toward my destination. To the east rises a great mass of mountain— huge, rounded, dissected by drainages, pocketed by slides and slumps, painted by patches of shrubs and bands of trees, and veiled by blue sky. The air here is unpolluted. The horizon shows no yellowing, just the fading of dark blue at zenith to lighter and lighter shades of natural blue.

The Nahtuk River enters the Alatna at a wide spot. There is no wind; there are no rustling leaves. All is calm except for the splash of water over stones. The small Nahtuk pours its endless flow into the accumulation of all the rivers from farther upstream that compose the Alatna. I can hear trickling sounds far upstream, from a riffle, a small waterfall, or several braids of water bounding over a stony riverbed. The valley narrows here. Limestone hills, the gray and whitish sediments of ancient sealife, are on both sides and come almost right to the river. Cliffs take form—not high, but enclosing and canyonlike—and the river straightens up and flows right through them. It is an incredible stretch of river, with the gap of the valley far ahead and the isolated mountains jutting toward the evening sky. The streamside is lined with forests of tall spruce, and the landscape is reflected in slightly blurred images on the water.

I pass an old cabin just beyond the Nahtuk River, but the Alatna flow is so swift here that I do not stop to look at it. I wonder what it would have been like to live here alone all winter trapping furred mammals. The evening sets in slowly, dimming the area. The limestone is almost bare of hillside vegetation, and I stop on a sandy riverside shore where a small ridge separates the Alatna River from Takahula Lake.

I tie up *Blueberry* and grab my sleeping bag to bring it onto shore, but it weighs about twenty pounds. When I open the drawstring, water pours out. I panic, and hang the bag up in a tree. The wonder of synthetic fibers shows through as the water drains from the bag as soon as I hang it up. I carry my pack onto shore and open the top. Oi gewalt! Everything is soggy and swollen. My heart goes out as I think the worst for a moment. Maybe it all will mold and I will be foodless. I had thought that when my raft floated away from the log jam the worst was over, but now it seems that the worst has persisted all day and I just did not recognize it.

I empty everything out of my pack to survey the damage. Even though I had packed everything in two plastic bags, the jostling of the past weeks and miles must have weakened the bags, for they all have leaked. The cornmeal and wheat flour are wet, solid masses and the rice and barley are swollen. They look ruined. My granola looks like a soggy bunch of overcooked and cooled oatmeal, a tasteless, textureless mass. And the peanuts—I didn't know peanuts could swell up and be so soft and undesirable.

I roll over on my back and look up at the evening skies with despair. "But the damage has been done," I say to myself. "Get up and undo it." I collect lots of wood, build a big fire, and get to work frying out the soggy food. I spoon the wheat and cornmeal into my frying pan over the fire, stir the mixture constantly, and in no time it is dry. I gently heat the plastic bags to dry them, then I repackage the works. I try heating the rice and barley in similar fashion, but I can see that it will take a lot of time. I spread a large sheet of thick aluminum foil on the sand, put rocks around the edge to hold it down, and spread my rice and barley as thin as I can on top of it. There is a gentle breeze, and I hope they can begin to dry. I do not know what to do with the peanuts, so I open the bag and spread them out with the rice.

I spoon the granola into little patties and fry them until they are crisp. The brown sugar I had saved also is wet and most of it has dissolved, but I use some to sweeten the granola back to palatable quality. I end up with a stack of little oat cakes that are not nearly so exciting as the granola I had started out with. I try the peanuts again, heating them in the pan and sprinkling salt on them. Bland food seems repulsive to me now, and I know that even a bit of salt or sugar will render these washed foods decent for my hungry self.

While some of these things are heating, I look deeper into my pack. All my clothing is soaked, so I hang it all in the trees to dry. Then I think about other important things. My journal! I frantically dig for it, and find that the closed design of the book has left the pages wet but readable. I grit my teeth as I open my map case and lay the merely dampened maps out to dry. They are okay. Then the killer. If I had any energy left to cry, I would. My camera and binoculars are full of water, which has permeated the seals. They have been turned into useless weight instead of fine instruments. What a waste. I won't be able to look at another bird or mountain in the distance. I won't be able to take another photograph. And the film in the camera is probably ruined, too. I check my other rolls of exposed film, and find that their waterproof containers are truly waterproof. Hallelujah! Something has survived the flood.

I work with the fire for many hours and dry and clean up most of the mess. As I hold my sleeping bag up to the fire, carefully drying out the nylon and edges, I think about the day. My pride is shot, but I have repaired it, and my confidence will return. There will be no more log jams for me, no more wet experiences. I had not expected the first day to offer such trauma. But it is over. What is lost is lost. I crawl into my semidry sleeping bag and squirm damply until it warms up. I look up at the gray sky, and I know the sun will be up in a short while. The mountains are still, standing as they have stood for thousands of years, but this night is special. I am with them tonight, and they calm me. The flood of disaster evaporates from my drained mind. I am on the sands of this shore, relaxed by the soft sounds of the flowing river by my side. I drift into sleep, thinking of the pristine miles of earth I have seen today.

August 2

I get a late start this morning after having spent so many hours drying out everything and restoring my faith in my river-riding abilities. The damage was much greater than I had imagined, and now I fight with myself to be strong enough to get on down the river. I can call it quits now and wait at Takahula for a plane to pass by so I perhaps can catch a ride, but I decide to go ahead, trust myself, and use my developing skills for safely riding my raft.

First, I hike over the ridge to Takahula Lake to do some fishing. The forest is open, with blueberry patches and meadows of tussocks. To the north, huge barren Takahula Mountain rises from the lake. Other more distant mountains and valleys are all around. The hills are forested, sporting the dark green of spruce, and the light green of birches, with continuous rolling carpets of delicate vegetation beneath the trees.

The lake is big and looks as if it is deep and full of trout. I cast my flies out across the water, but I cannot cast out to where I can see a drop-off to deeper waters. I hike farther around and from some rocks cast my black flies as far as I can, but still no luck. It has been many, many days since I have eaten any meat, probably the longest I have gone without meat in my life—all the days hiking down the fishless Kutuk, raft building on the murky Alatna, losing again at fishless Arrigetch and here at no-luck Takahula. Many days of meager rations, supplemented only by finger-dug Eskimo potatoes and juicy blueberries, have left me craving fish. I know I can catch some, but I guess the distribution of fish is very spotty, and I have not been in the right spot at the right time. I still have a lot to learn about fish finding in these new waters, and my hunger and my needs will help me learn to satisfy myself.

I hike back from the lake to the sandy shore of the Alatna

River. I pack up *Blueberry* and cast off for another try at the river. It is a still, blue-sky, warm, nearly cloudless day. The water takes its time, and the raft flows as the river flows, as any particle of water flows down this channel of fluids collected from these mountains. It goes no slower than any other drop; no faster either, although at any one time some drops move in the current while others are caught in the eddies. It all evens out with time, and my long spruce pole helps me keep the raft in swifter waters as much as possible. I consider the raft one of the most rapidly moving entities on the river. It is nice to know, because the river is so slow at times that I feel good knowing that my craft is going as fast as this river will allow.

I stop soon and cut some spruce from a fallen tree and build a new, larger seat. It is composed of two poles running across the back part of the raft, then two poles running at ninety-degree angles to these and on top of them to form a square frame. Then I put three more poles across the top of this—a total of three high from the raft logs—and tie it all together. On the back part of this rack, I tie my pack, then I tie my sleeping bag on the front of my pack so I can have a soft back-rest. I put my feet up on the center cross log and in this fashion, I float away again, comfortable, relaxed, and dry.

There is very little wind today and no mosquitoes out over the water. But the huge biting flies are around me constantly. They make huge circles around me like hawks circling their prey, and then pass close, "buzzzzzzzzzz," and again, "buzzzzzzzz," finding a spot to land. I swat, rarely getting the satisfaction of killing one. It is like this all day. It is warm, almost hot, and I like to sit without clothing on. I have not felt the sun this strongly on my skin except for my face all summer. Now, stretched out on the river this sunny day, I am hounded by biting flies. But I enjoy the naked weather in spite of them.

A fleet of ducks—a mama and seven little ones—crosses the river in front of me. Their panic at seeing me is funny. They turn downstream, paddling as fast as they can, with mama leading and looking back occasionally, then paddling more furiously. She sees me following and goes the route of quickest flight, downstream. Soon they duck into an eddy at riverside and swim under an overhanging alder. They stay hidden as I pass, peering out at me from between leaves. I look back and see them leisurely swimming off across the river, just as when I had found them.

The river has many small islands and bends and the deepest channel of water zigzags within the river and is not always easy to find. When I come upon a spot where the water branches into two channels, I try to decide where the main flow is going and then pole into it. Many times I pole into the more shallow channel before realizing that I am wrong. Usually I am already so close to the diverging point that the water is too shallow for my logs to float and the current deposits me there. My error. I get off to push and pull.

I am learning that the design of *Blueberry* lets it follow the main flow of water. When I relax and let it choose the course, it does quite well. My job is to keep it away from sweepers and out of eddies. This keeps me busy and content, for if I had nothing to do, I would go crazy knowing that I was at the mercy of the river and that I was in no way helping my progress.

I stay on the river as long as possible and regain confidence that I can handle anything. The warmth of the day fades as the sun goes behind one of the high limestone mountains to the west. I pull off and find a perfect campsite. The forests are becoming warmer and more homey all the time. Here, stands of white spruce reach high up toward the graying evening skies. It feels so good to sit among tall trees. Alders and willows form a ten-foot-high shrub understory, and blueberries, bearberries, Eskimo potatoes, and horsetails cover the ground. Old fallen logs and stumps are covered with lichens and extensive moss patches. It is a colorful, comfortable evening home.

I eat my grains sitting on the bank, looking back up the valley to the ridges and hills and mountains I have passed this day. A few bank swallows fly by, darting back and forth above the water, catching insects. These are the first swallows I have seen and they give me an added feeling of southern worlds. With this warmth still inside me, I find my sleeping bag.

Arctic tern

AUGUST 3

I awake startled. The sun is not quite up over the mountains, but the valley is light, and I can faintly see into the forest. The sound of screaming in the not too distant hills scares me. I know it is a wolf or wolves, and the echoing in the otherwise silent valley is piercing. It sounds as if the creature is next to me. I need not fear wolves; I know that. They are not usually predators of humans. But now, alone, I fear them. I leap out of my sleeping bag, throw everything together and onto *Blueberry,* and cast off in a matter of minutes. On the river I am safe. Being alone brings on funny feelings and at times causes me to fear things that would not normally disturb me. I realize that I even got onto my raft before eating breakfast, which is definitely not my normal behavior.

The river surface is absolutely still. The current is slow and again all is silent. My heart, too, slows its beat. An occasional "chick-a-dee-dee" from a boreal chickadee in the streamside alders embraces the morning stillness. I keep my breathing as inaudible as possible to bathe in the essence of morning silence.

The day quickly warms as the sun moves above the ridge and fills the valley with its rays. I spend hours gazing at mountain after mountain, studying each ridge, valley, and ribbon of trees. Birches are bright green, splashed upon the hills in dazzling color. They mingle with tall white spruce which poke from the closed birch forest like spires and are now touched by sun. The mountains here are composed of folded limestone sediments, and the bare cliffs and exposed rock layers jut into the arctic air. Every inch of every mile is different. Every part of the riverbank I look at is a unique jumble of trees — willows in clumps with fifteen-foot-high branches and junglelike vegetation and brush that would be hell to hike in with a pack. I am glad I am rafting. From the river, the whole landscape seems mountainous and rolling, with hardly a flat spot even along the river.

I pass a mountain of uptilted bedrock, the strata of which is all exposed. It is raw and sheer, and the river meandering back and forth takes me close and then farther away for many different veiws. I float through continual meanders, slowly winding snakelike back and forth across and down the valley. Some meanders again take me in the reverse direction. Each one brings the sight of eroded banks with fallen trees and turfs of vegetation hanging over the banks like long, dangling tongues. The main flow of water is always against these banks on the outside of bends, and I dodge fallen trees that lie in the water in these areas. Coming across the river with the current and looking downstream at the array of sweepers with trash piled up is quite scary. I know I must negotiate each one. On the opposite side of the river, the dynamics of river erosion produce fascinating contrasting effects. Huge sand and gravel bars are formed by slower currents depositing rocks and sediments. Horsetails form extensive stands of lime green vegetation here, and in the brilliant sunlight, shine like velvet. Balsam poplars grow higher in the gravel desposits. Around every bend, I can see this pattern of bank erosion and sand and gravel bars, with the poplars giving way to spruce as the site stability increases.

In a long, calm stretch, I see a small brown object swimming toward me. At first I am unsure what it is, then it lifts its broad flat tail, slaps the water, and is gone under the surface — a typical beaver stunt, warning other beavers of some alarming intruder. In another stretch, the raft floats close to the bank and I hear some rustling in the willows. One willow bush shakes violently, and then another, and another, each closer to the river. Finally, a brown, squat, waddling form ambles to the water and slides in. It looks up, sees me, slaps the water with another beaver warning, dives, and is gone.

The day stays warm, with a few cumulus clouds moving and building. The wind picks up and blows strongly and steadily from the south. This is a new obstacle, the wind. The raft and I provide so much friction and resistance that we are pushed across the river in a crosswind and slowed to a near standstill in a stretch where the wind comes head on. It is amazing at first to think that the gentle wind can do that. Soon, however, I realize that the wind is no friend and will fight my progress down this river. Coming around a meander, the raft is blown against the shore. I pole against the bottom where I can reach it to push the raft into the current and keep the craft moving downstream. On the outside of such meanders, the bank has been gouged in many places by heavy spring runoff. A little whirlpool eddy forms in these areas, and the wind likes to force my raft into them. I try to pole out of them, but the water is too deep and I cannot touch bottom. I learn to paddle out, using my pole as a kayak paddle, sweeping on one side, then the other, and this moves the raft, slowly, hardly, barely. I would relax and let the wind do its business, but I know it would take me twice as long to cover these miles if I didn't help guide the raft.

Lunch today is a treat I have looked forward to all day. Just before I lifted my usual cornmeal and whole wheat biscuits from the frying pan last night, I spread a spoonful of brown sugar on each one and let it melt. As the biscuits cooled, the sugar hardened to form a frosting. Sweetness is something I have nearly forgotten and it seems new and different. I savor every bite of this meal.

A pair of arctic terns are on the river up ahead, which tells me there are small fish (which they eat) in the water. These terns are placid compared with the ones I experienced on Chandler and Amiloyak lakes. They dart in the air above me, but there are no dives, swoops, threats, or screeches, and their visit is a pleasurable one.

All day the clouds are wisps and shells and smears along the blue, blue sky. When the raft floats along a tree-sheltered bank, protecting me from the wind, and the current is good, I know this is the way to travel, smoothly, constantly flowing past inch after inch of wild land.

I come to a major conclusion after being frustrated many times by the wind. I reason that the river and the elements that shape this environment are big and strong. I can't effectively fight them, so I relax and enjoy the expansive country.

The raft seems like an old horse to me now. It knows the

path; it knows the easiest way home. It may be slow, but true and steady are its virtues. Many times I can pick out the deep channels even though the surface water all seems to be similar, but sometimes I find myself fighting the raft to move across the river to what I think is a better current or deeper channel, and then end up dragging myself off the gravel, or scraping bottom. The raft usually knows the easiest way. Of course, *Blueberry* makes mistakes, too. In one area, the river splits around a small sandbar and I think I should pole over one way or the other as it looks as if we are heading right for the bar. Since I cannot decide which is the best way to go, I let *Blueberry* decide and I wait. We move right toward the bar, and the water becomes shallower and shallower. When *Blueberry* finally goes to the right, the water is too shallow. We settle out as if we were a stone, sitting still, high, and too dry. Then I get off and try to drag the beast back into deeper water.

Evening and the time to get off the river arrive when the sun sinks behind the peaks. Chill comes quickly as the air cools and settles into this lowest part of the valley. I find a spot just after a broad meander where the water is deep, but not swift, close to shore. This way, I can bring the raft right to shore and step off without getting my feet wet. The forest is close enough to the river so I can tie the raft to a tree, preventing a rise in the water level from floating my transportation away.

It gets darker and darker each evening as the season moves farther from summer solstice. Sunset this evening is a glow of orange the likes of which I have not seen on this trip. All northern clouds erupt in fiery color, and the shades and tones of evening persist throughout dinnertime. I am along the last mountains in the Brooks Range. To the west, a tall dissected mass runs east and west. It is a huge massif, as big as some Rocky Mountain ranges, with many valleys and lakes. From here on, there will be only the hills that I see to the south. But now, all fades together into gray, and I am left with the faint glow of light on the northern horizon.

AUGUST 4

Another day in the life of a river rider. I gather a cupful of blueberries to have with my breakfast and another small bagful to munch on as I float. The last section of mountain river meanders are painfully slow, but soon I am out of the mountains and into a small bedrock canyon that is not deep, but the river narrows here and becomes very quick. The current moves the raft rapidly, as I have always wanted it to move.

In one broader stretch, a small airplane, flying low, passes overhead, then turns and circles for a few loops. It dips a right wing, then a left to signal, "Hello, how are you?" I wave my hat wildly, happy to see humans. Then it flies on, and its sound fades into the sound of the river world. Human contact like this is so fragmentary and unpredictable. Sometimes, it seems as if this infinite country and waterway has swallowed me up and there is no other reality, no other place or people on earth—just me and the endless river.

When the current is slow, the encompassing land seems all too big, as if I can never reach the end, as if my destiny is to float slowly, ever so slowly, for the rest of my life down this river. The shore creeps by, and I note progress in passing each spruce, each large stone, each unusual feature. I can sit back, soothed in the serene environment of calm water, surrounded by reflected figures of streamside vegetation, hills and mountains, and the blue sky. I can be calm one second, then feel an outburst of frustration. I need to move through this sleepy stretch of river; I need to get down this river! My pole sends ripples across the calm water, small splashes are heard, the perfect reflections of landscapes in the water dissolve, and the magical aspects of this vast land, its grand and expansive untouched character, become unwanted features. I do not appreciate any scenes, my love for the wilds evaporates. I hate the huge distances I must travel, and I want only easy passage, though I now know that is anything but easy. As slowly as I am going, it is almost no passage.

Later, the water moves swiftly and the raft really scoots along. At times like this, I wish the feeling could last forever. The instant acceleration of rapid water, the rushing I feel, the speed, are thrilling compared with the lull of calm water. I feel as if I am white-water rafting, in a primitive way.

I come upon a stretch where a riffle accelerates the water into chops. The channel narrows, and sounds of churning are heard everywhere. Chops increase in size, and there is foam, spray, and white water. My eyes widen, but I am not frightened. Many of the rivers flowing south from the Brooks Range have rapids that would be too dangerous for *Blueberry* and me. But natives of the region traditionally floated down the Alatna, Reed, and Mauneluk rivers on log rafts similar to mine, and so I have no fear of encountering treacherous rapids or falls. I try to move more into the middle of the channel, but the raft is in the grips of the current and the friction of the logs on the water makes it impossible for me to move it. I use my strongest pole to keep the raft directed straight into the current, but find that the friction differential of the raft is doing it for me, and so I enjoy the fast pace without having to work extra for it.

After this first rapid, the water continues fast, streaming and churning. Up ahead the canyon walls are vertical and the river bends very sharply to the right. I can hear the roar of rapidly moving water, pounding against the large, rounded rocks that stick up here and there above the flow. I think I will have problems dodging the rocks, but the strength of the flow guides me around them as long as I am pointing straight into the current.

I get into the rapid at the bend and stand up with my legs spread, braced, to enjoy the change of pace. This fast water jostles the raft, as the logs hardly bend or absorb any shock, but we flow through the churn with ease. The turbulence causes water to be above the top of the logs, and I am standing several inches below the highest point of water. I smile from the sheer joy of swift movement.

After the rapid, the river slows but continues at a quicker pace than in the meanders. The hills that surround the river are awash with the remnants of a recent large fire. Pink fireweed blossoms on waist-tall stalks are growing like grasses on the great plains, one plant growing right next to another. I can see pink for miles and miles.

I pole the raft over to the shore and tie it to a large rock. Then I hike across the gravel flats and up the steep hillside onto the level, rolling plateau and hill country into which the Alatna cuts. I am surrounded by small, dead, burned trees. Some stand black and charred, some lie in heaps. The colors of skeletal spruce and pink fireweed against the blue sky and the shapes of hills and mountains make an unending pattern. I break a fireweed stalk near its base and split it lengthwise with my thumbnail. Inside the stem is an edible cortex tissue, and though it is not sweet or juicy, it is good food. I do not take much time to eat these stems, because I really have stopped here to look for blueberries. A native woman in Bettles told me that once there was a big fire near the village, and for several years after that the blueberries were incredibly lush, with abundant fruit. But the fire here must have been many years ago, because plants such as blueberries that have come up from surviving roots have been dwarfed by the wild, proliferating fireweed that almost totally blankets the land surface. I am not disappointed, though, by the lack of blueberries, for I can find them elsewhere, and the experience of this charred, dry-looking, shadeless area has been worth stopping for anyway.

I start down the slope, and in some areas of bare soil, I find wild roses. The flowers have come and gone and the ripening fruit, the hips, stand red and oblong on the bushes. I pick a handful and pop them into my mouth one by one, softening the skin with saliva and spitting out the hard seeds before chewing the fruit. These also are not particularly flavorful, but they are rich in vitamin C, and are fresh, wild-growing members of this environment, and so I love them. There also are scattered raspberry bushes, but they have few berries. I suck each one with my eyes closed to savor its rare and delightful taste. These are the first raspberries I have seen all summer.

I hike down to the gravel along the river and find another plant that I am seeing for the first time on this trip—wild chives. They are everywhere! I scream with the joy of discovery and start prying at the ground with my knife. I loosen up a bunch, cut off the jumble of roots, and wash the sand from the bulbs. Then I peel off the dead layers and taste the morsels. Wow, they are potent, and what a resource—all the onions I want to pick right here at riverside. I clean enough to fill a plastic sack and tuck them into my pack to garnish many a day's meal.

I hop back on my raft and pole into the swift current. The feel of movement, the feel of the force of gravity upon water as the river grabs the raft, is exhilarating. Off we go down a few miles of bending channel, alternating between calm and briskly moving water. The hillsides are painted with the reds and pinks of fireweed and with blotches of other green pioneering plants. Strips of live, mature spruce linger here and there, having somehow been spared from the scorching heat that took away all leaves, branches, and life, and burned the soils anchoring the roots. These spruce live as islands, remnants of an obliterated forest in a sea of pioneer fireweed and skeletal spruce. They are providing the valuable seed that will reforest these slopes.

Far off I hear another roaring, and after rounding a ninety-degree bend, I come upon a rapid larger than the last two. I stand up, ready to navigate the raft, but the raft knows what to do. It turns the corner with the current and heads directly into the churning water. The rapid is like a riffle blown out of proportion, with each chop one to two feet high and white with foam of bursting bubbles. I get wet streaming through this section, but I am laughing, enjoying the river in a different way than I had before these fast stretches. Through the rapid we go toward a high hill that is cloaked in spruce and paper birches. All greens shine in the strong midday sunshine.

I am now between the Helpmejack Hills to the west and the Alatna Hills to the east. They reach several thousand feet in height, with alpine tundra vegetation at their tops. In a slow stretch, another airplane flies by. It flies low just as the other airplane had done. It is so exciting for me to be the attraction that they come to see. It makes me remember the thrilling aspects of this trip, and obscures my memory of the tedious parts.

A calm stretch after some riffles causes me to lie back, stretch my feet and breathe a sigh. All that surrounds me sifts by continuously on a serene note. The afternoon brings a few clouds and strong winds from the south. The wind produces waves on the water, and in long, broad stretches of river, I feel as if this is a lake on a windy day. I remember back to when the current swept the raft along at a steady, calming, rapid pace. Now there are calm stretches, one after another, where the raft hardly moves and the wind almost pushes it backward. Where the Malamute Fork of the Alatna River joins the main Alatna, the river really broadens out, and the current dies. The raft does not move. The wind is right in my face, and the countryside stands still except for the flapping trees and leaves and the waves that move upriver. How can I be calm with no current, no movement? I will not let the wind direct my life. So, I get off and pull *Blueberry* downriver about a hundred yards, then I hop back on and the raft floats slowly away. This time, the raft makes a bit of progress, though certainly without much speed. The river bends in almost every part, and luckily not many stretches face directly into the wind.

Around a bend, crosswinds push the raft constantly toward the shore. I push out into the center of the river with my pole, and pick up a bit of current as the wind pushes the raft shoreward again. It is a constant task to stay in the current. I again pull the raft when I cannot stand sitting as the wind holds the raft in a static position. I doubt that pulling does much to increase my speed or distance. All it accomplishes is to increase my pulse and give me a tension release, a way to expend my pent-up energy and frustration. If only I could control myself better at these times. If only I could let the environment be the boss and play by its rules. But no, I have to have everything my way. I have to have current when I want it, calmness when I want it, instead of enjoying it all when it comes. Most of the time, I can enjoy it as it appears. It's just when the river and my ideas conflict that I become frustrated, because nature always wins in the wilderness.

In a nice stretch later in the evening, I come to a ninety-degree bend, with a steep wall on the inside and a sandbar on the outside. As I come around the corner, I notice a young moose, a yearling, standing at the riverside. It looks up at me, stares for a minute, looks left, then right, wheels around, and runs a few steps away from me. Then it stops, looks back over its shoulder, wheels toward me, and walks back up to the riverside. It seems that it simultaneously is frightened and curious. The insects are out and the moose shakes its head constantly, flopping its big ears back and forth. At this corner, the river moves fast, curving back around to the right. The moose cannot let me out of its sight. It walks down the bank as I float, and we look at each other for quite awhile. But slowly the river takes me beyond the curve, and I leave the moose alone upon the shore, perhaps never again to see a two-footed creature.

I make it to the first big bend on the next map, the Hughs quadrangle. Survey Pass, my companion map since the Agiak Creek country, is put away. The Brooks Range is far to the north now. The evening sun is low in the sky, sinking behind the mountains to the northwest. The southern slopes of the range appear dry, exposed, and barren. They are high, and it is hard to fathom that they run as far as can be imagined east to west, and as far as I have traveled from north to south. A massive bunch of folded earth stretches before me and fades with evening.

The Alatna Hills catch the last yellowed rays of direct sunlight. They are high hills with fingers of treelike vegetation creeping up the deeply dissected valleys and gullies of slopes. Above that, the tundra is cloaked in a golden hue of dried sedges and herbs, already gathering fall colors, and shining as the last drops of day are bestowed upon it.

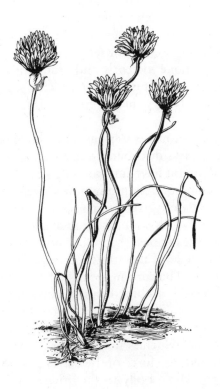

Wild chives

August 5

The calm, cloudless evening is as cold as I remember experiencing so far this summer, and I crouch deep into my sleeping bag all night to keep warm.

I have weird dreams about dark, deep forests and mystical encounters in my wanderings, and decide that I have been entertained by the fortunes of Tolkien's trilogy characters too much this month. Now I am dreaming my own fantasy journeys and jumping from wild episode to wild episode. It is hard enough to retain memory of my civilized sanity out here day after day when I work with the basic premises of nature and consciousness, but when I have to wake to a clouded mind full of unknown ideas and questions, it makes me unsure where I really am physically. The questions of why I am here begin anew, unleashed by self upon self.

My day starts none too early and I hit good current, much the same as yesterday. It is another enticing summer morning with clear views of every shining entity in this arena of life and objects.

One long area of fast water has many huge rocks, half the size of automobiles, distributed randomly in and around it. The current does not have time to braid new channels around each rock. I come barreling down this stretch, poling when possible to modify my given course, but I am moving too fast to pole effectively. As soon as I touch bottom and start to push off, I am already past that point, and can give but a little push. In the middle of the stretch, I head directly toward a huge round rock. The current seems to be taking me right toward it, and there is nothing I can do. I paddle with my pole ends, but bang, I hit it head on and it throws me forward. The force of the river starts to take the rear end to the left, pivoting around the front, which is not moving. Before the rear end can swing around, the force of the current is trying to flip the raft! I shift my whole body to the other side in a desperate lunge and almost fall over the edge. The current lifts the raft higher until it is almost vertical, but then the rear end is far enough around so that the raft moves off of the rock and lies down flat in the water again. But then we are going down the river backward, and there are more rocks below. I can't turn the raft around, and I won't turn it sideways in the current because if the raft hits a rock broadside, it really might flip.

I do not think the raft can break. The logs are strong and flexible, and it would take an amazing shock to shatter one. It is almost like an unbreakable vehicle, tightly lashed and made of nature's finest materials. I only fear getting hung up and not being able to get off, or flipping over and losing gear. That would be the worst thing that could happen. But the raft gets past the rocks and I turn it around.

After another nice fast stretch, the river bends ninety degrees and, at the elbow, comes up against an arching bedrock dome. Creeping slowly up to the symmetrical structure, I am enchanted by its vegetative character. Tall spruce trees grow like spires through the continuous broadleaf canopy of paper birches. The face of the hill is very steep, and thousands of white trunks grow upright upon the hill. It looks like a paradise of lush vegetation, and I smile in wonderment. The river broadens into a small, still, lakelike area. The hill raises straight from the pool, with bare rock exposed for thirty or forty feet before becoming vegetated. It is silent. I feel as if I am in a deep canyon of still waters. I cast with my fly rod and lay the floating line upon the mirrorlike water. But I see no fish. I paddle up to the front of the pool. A tiny stream comes down from the hill, and in a tiny cove it falls as a tiny waterfall. It is a misty, green cove with a canopy of alders that filters the sunlight, letting only green pass. It is a wondrous little nook, the kind I would like to crawl into and dream effervescent, splashing dreams for the rest of the day. But I only gaze into it, taking the sight with me forever. Perhaps I can enter it in the weeks to come when I close my eyes, needing to be back here in just such a place.

I float slowly into more rapidly moving waters, and the

stream breaks into two braids. The force of the current takes the raft down the left channel. The shallow water allows me to see the cobblestone riverbed filled with rocks from so many conceivable sources, rounded by years of wear by water, gathered in just this array at just this fragile moment in history when I pass fleetingly, wondering about the continuous processes of change.

The other channel joins us and there is a long stretch of shallow, swift water. Everywhere are small hills of birches and areas of low relief with stunted black spruce.

Ecological patterns of succession from flood plain to forest are well illustrated here. The river is a constant force, eroding the outside of meanders and depositing sediments on the inside of meanders. On the inside of bends, goose grass and fireweed and willows are pioneers on new sediments, balsam poplars replace them in more stable areas, and finally spruce are present again on deposits that are probably several hundred years old. Each bend or area of migrating river shows these patterns. It is constantly in action, a flow of change here and everywhere.

Soon I pass Rockybottom Creek, which comes bubbling down from the Alatna Hills. I decide to stop and try my luck at fishing again. Grabbing my fly rod with a black gnat, I head to the thin ribbon of water. The sands around the stream are marked with bear tracks. I look around me suddenly in a panic, but just as quickly turn my thoughts back to fish. The clear stream flows rapidly over a bed of small stones. Trees have fallen this way and that in it and pools have formed. I whip out my fly and catch a tiny grayling. I laugh, holding it out of the water for just a second, squinting to see it. I then release it and cast my fly along the edge of a fallen spruce tree. At the tail end of the tree, I yank out a ten-inch fish. It's not big, but I haven't had meat for a long time, so I keep it. My next cast is up to what was the top of the tree. A fish rises in the shade and takes my fly. I set the hook, the fish tugs, and I see its side flash in the sunlight. Wow! It's huge. I think it is a salmon at first, but after a few runs up and down the pool, I see it is a grayling. I pull it in to shore and still smiling, cast again. The mature grayling are all about seventeen inches long, far larger than any I have caught yet on this trip. One fish really gives me a fight, running down the river a hundred feet and causing me to take up chase. I end up with four fish and secure some delicious meals for two days. This place has become an immediate love: Rockbottom has broken my fishless spell.

I walk back to my raft through the forest instead of along the river and walk into an amazing blueberry patch. I laugh again. It seems when things go right, everything goes right. The bushes here are absolutely loaded with berries and I collect enough to keep me happily munching for several hours.

Back on the river, I approach a tiny cabin in a straight stretch near the Helpmejack Lakes and pole over to the riverside to see if anyone lives there now. It is empty and locked up. A big stack of wood is cut, and I think perhaps it is used either for fall hunting or winter trapping.

The river soon goes through another set of meanders but the wind is not so violent as it was yesterday. Meanders do not get me very far on the map, but if I could pull them straight like a string, they would total a long distance. I negotiate three full meanders here, each almost a complete circle. These meanders are not so slow as those in the mountains. There are riffles in some stretches, and the flow is continuous. In stretch after stretch the river curves against bedrock walls that rise into hills of birches. A pair of goshawks screech at me in one stretch, where I see the effects of another fire.

Before I leave these meanders, an airplane flies by. It circles, I wave my hat, and it slows. I scream, "No, I'm okay. Don't land." But it lines itself up and lands on the river, stopping about a hundred yards ahead. The pilot gets out and pulls the plane around so its tail is toward land. He then hikes into the forest and returns with an aluminum canoe over his shoulder. He lays it upon a float and starts lashing it down just as I float up. I get off the raft and pull it toward the plane and say,

"Hi." His name is Don. He rolls a cigar in his mouth and tells me he is a pilot out of Bettles and has come to pick up these canoes. Now I remember that David Schmitz, the guide I had met in Arrigetch, had told me of canoes that he had left down here. The pilot had heard of me in Bettles, as there was a note up in the lodge for pilots to keep an eye out for a traveler— me. We talk about places I have been to, and he wonders what kind of big game I have seen in the area I have passed through. I ask him what he has seen, as flying gives a whole different perspective. He thinks the raft would be slow, and I say jovially, "It's slow as slow." He pulls two paddles out of the canoe, gives them to me, and says I can probably build a pair of oars from them. They are just what I need. I ask to see his map so I can trace the lower portion of the Alatna River, as I do not have the connecting topographical map that I need. He gives me an old tattered aviation map that suits my purposes perfectly, and I am very grateful. He tells me that there are some Indian fishing camps down the river, and I get ideas about catching salmon. He has to go, but first asks me whether I would like a ride to Bettles. He knows how slow this river can get. I think of the wild and adventurous parts of this day and I say, "No, thanks." He says, "I didn't think so."

He motors upriver, then heading downstream, fills the valley with the accelerating sounds of an aircraft. Soon the noise is gone, and I am on the river again, floating in the quiet afternoon air. The memory of this chance encounter is all I have except for the wooden paddles in my hand.

The paddles help incredibly. I use only one, paddling as if I were in a canoe. The raft, however, is not very responsive to a single stroke. I make up for it in numbers of strokes, and I find it is much easier to move in the current with a paddle than with my pole. The day stays clear and calm, and the evening becomes cloudless. I pull off to camp near a big eddy on the outside of a meander. I start a fire and get my rice and barley cooking, and I go back to the river for more fishing.

I hear a great churning splash about thirty feet upriver and cannot understand what it is. I have heard similar noises many times before while on the raft and have thought they must be beaver. But now I see a long, slender fish swim by right in front of me. A northern pike! My eyes bulge, and I stand motionless until it passes. It looks as if it is about two feet long. I run up to my pack and put on a silver spinner. I start casting and, on the third cast, hook the fish. My pulse is speeding, and I can feel the sides of my head swell in anticipation. The pike thrashes for a second and then my line goes limp and weightless. The pike has bitten through my line, and I learn that I must use a piece of wire behind the lure. I have only one more lure and decide to save it. I put on a fly and cast it out for fun, and as soon as it hits the calm surface, a huge grayling leaps into the air and takes it. This fish is even bigger than the grayling from Rockybottom.

I put two fish into my rice and barley to have for dinner tonight, fry up some wild onions in margarine, and mix up two teaspoons of instant lemon pudding that David Schmitz had given to me. When the pudding starts to harden, I add a cup of blueberries and let the pudding cool. It is a dinner fit for a king. I fry up the rest of the fish to have with breakfast and lunch tomorrow.

As evening dims my world, the moon comes up as a glowing ball over the Alatna Hills. Bands of light reflect off the silent, seemingly still river. I hope tomorrow will be like this day has been.

August 6

I am visited in the first minutes of my float by a pair of ravens. Sometimes these birds give notice of their presence by loud "gronking" sounds. Sometimes there are no resonating voices, just the whooshing beat of wings in the air above and the silhouetted forms passing by. Sometimes they circle curiously and land in a tree. But today there is no diversion, no sound—just the movement of forms that speaks of raven.

Below Helpmejack Creek, the river is extravagantly fast. It flows through small bedrock hills, and there are no meanders. For every river mile, a mile is moved straight across the map. It is extremely good for my motivation, gaining these chunks of territory so easily. There are many shallow areas and I learn to stand up when I recognize one. Then I can see areas where small deeper channels gather to flow over the bedrock. Poling into one, I get in the flow and float right through the shallows.

To satisfy my blueberry lust, I know that I must find a stand or an area of white spruce trees. White spruce are taller, fuller trees than black spruce, which tend to grow on poorly drained, boggy soils. The latter are spindly, small, crooked, seemingly sickly trees. Blueberries grow best where the white spruce are not really tall or growing closely together, which allows ample sunlight to get through to allow the growth of sweet berries. The area also is usually vegetated with alders, some willows, and lots of Labrador tea. It is so nice to be floating along craving berries, and then to see a stand that looks just right, get off the river, step into the forest, and be surrounded by luscious berries. Ah, the great feeling of understanding my surroundings.

Just downriver, I see a flock of Canada geese on the gravel bank. They honk in low voices as if conversing with each other. A few become restless and start walking. Soon all of them are up and scooting along the bank. Although they are waddling, they move fast, and soon disappear into the forest to be seen and heard no more. Many geese at this time of the year molt and are flightless for a few weeks. These probably are flightless. I do not stop to pursue them.

This seems to be a day of wildlife. Two sharp-shinned hawks visit me, soaring from tree to tree, screeching at me as they protect their territory. These are smaller birds with longer tails than the goshawks. I also see several marsh hawks, which are low-flying, medium-sized hawks with a white fluffy patch of feathers on the rump. They hunt for small rodents along the river and lowlands.

Toward evening I look for a small stream in hopes of fishing for grayling. There are many tiny tributaries that spill over the bank into the river with loud gurgling, splashing noises. Some of the main tributaries that enter from the hills are soundless. The mouth of a tributary that runs parallel to the river sometimes is hidden by a sandbar between the river and the tributary. The water from such a side stream enters the river slowly, and I have missed some streams because of it. Now I see what appears to be a stream and pole over toward shore. There is a sandbank with horsetails, their light, bright yellow color adorning the bank. It is called goose grass up here because geese love to eat it. From where I have landed the raft to the area upriver where I want to fish is about a hundred feet, and the goose grass in the area has been nibbled to nubbins, almost flush with the ground. Webbed footprints left during a muddy, rainy interval cover the ground, and feathers and droppings are everywhere in this home or evening inn of Canada geese. I walk barefooted to the side stream, and when I get there, I am immediately disappointed that it is merely a slough of shallow, almost standing water, with but a trickle of water entering it. I know grayling would never stand for it, but looking into the water, I see several long objects lying in the mud beneath the water. Pike! I go back to my raft and find my wire. I use about an eight-inch piece and attach a spinner to one end. At the other end, I form a loop of the wire, and to this I tie the leader that is tied to my floating line.

I sneak back to the slough, being as quiet and stealthy as

possible. I kneel down on the sand at the side of the slough and check to see that all the knots leading to my lure are secured. This is the only lure I have, and I do not want to lose it. When I am sure everything is tight, I strip out thirty feet of line. Since this is a fly line, I cannot cast my lure. I organize the line into a pile, and then throw the lure by hand across to the other side of the slough. Then, making a quick motion with my rod and reeling simultaneously as fast as possible, I pull the lure from the opposite bank and send it spinning, shining, flashing across the open water.

Almost immediately I see a large object dart toward my lure and seize it viciously. Jaws clamp down on the steel prey, and I feel the tug, as if a person were holding the line and tugging it from me. I give a sharp yank on the pole to set the cluster of barbed hooks deep in its plated jaw. The pike responds by leaping from the water and flailing its powerful head from side to side. It lands with a splash and swims up to the head of the slough as rapidly as it can. Flailing its head, flexing its strong body, thrusting its tail from side to side, it leaps from the shallow water, crashing back into the still surface again and again.

This continues for a few vigorous minutes, but the pike tires quickly. Pike are like sprinters—they have amazing energy for quick bursts, but they have no endurance. Soon the fish is belly up, and I drag it onto the shore and carry it back to my raft.

I slit open its stomach to see what it has eaten recently and find a small mouse, a small fish, and a moth—quite an array of local fauna. I pass a string down its mouth and out its gills, knot the string, and tow the fish behind the raft as I float on downriver. This is the largest fish I have caught so far, and I can't wait to taste it. I have been munching on pieces of grayling all day, left over from my catch at Rockybottom Creek yesterday. Still, my fish appetite is greatly aroused.

I float a little while longer and then choose a site where I can stop and prepare my feast. I start a fire and get a bed of glowing, hot coals going. I spread them out in a line while keeping my fire burning at one end. I then place my grill upon two rocks that are on either side of the coals and set the whole pike upon the grill. I keep feeding my fire and replenishing the coals under the pike to keep it cooking.

I intermittently collect blueberries and when I have a bagful, go about the task of piemaking. In a small aluminum dish that I had gotten from David Schmitz, I melt some margarine, then add flour until the mixture is thick and doughy. I flatten the dough with my fingers to form a thin crust on the bottom and sides of the dish. I cook this on the grill, and then add blueberries with some raisins to add sweetness and some more flour to soak up the berry juice and thicken it. When my rice is finished boiling, I cut raw onions into it and fry it in my skillet. While I dine on my delicious broiled pike and my rice, I put the pie inside my pot and cover it. I set it on the grill to bake just until it is heated and bubbling all the way through. This way, the sweet juices of ripe berries are fully exposed and mix with the succulent flavor of raisins. The combination, after cooling a little, is a pure expression of pie. Blueberry pie in blueberry land. What a meal this is. I can think of no finer things to eat anywhere than the wild products of the land I live with, mixed with a few basic foods of ancient civilized man that I carry with me. This is also a satisfying experience in self-sufficiency—finding the foods I need in the environment I live in. And it's also delicious.

The season for mosquitoes is almost over now, but the no-see-ums are thick in the forests. In the evening as the air cools, huge clouds of them form. They are not like mosquitoes, which just land on me and walk around a bit. These insects crawl up sleeves and pant legs, inside holes, down collars, and into ears. No repellent can be applied heavily enough to rid me of them entirely. Their bites are like pinpricks, and my legs are bitten all over. I wake up several times each night in fits of scratching. I grease my face with insect repellent before I lie down to sleep. If I take off my clothing before I get into my sleeping bag, I am covered with insects immediately and must jump up and down while rubbing my hands over my limbs.

Life is crazy with such pests. The only way to escape them is to sit on the side of a fire where the smoke is blowing toward me. My eyes water and I can hardly breathe, but there are no insects. I suffer through it, and most evenings as the temperature drops to its low point, the insects disappear. Then I am able to sleep without a head net, without predators lurking inches away. It is a pleasurable experience.

The evening is a bit warmer than past evenings have been. There appears to be some sort of an air mass to the south, a cloudy congestion at the horizon. I hope I am imagining it.

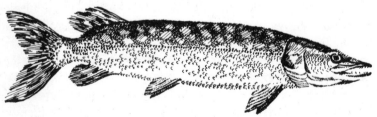

Northern pike

August 7

The day awakes with the cloud bank now overhead. It forms a low, gray ceiling, and the cool, damp feeling of moisture is upon my skin and penetrates deep into my bones. Brrrrr. I miss the sun already. The whole area receives no bright light, just dim filtered rays through the layers of clouds. The evening chill seems as if it will linger through the day, and I know the sun will not appear.

I rise, quickly gather my gear and jump on *Blueberry*. I am anxious to be on the river and making progress before the weather becomes wetter. Being on the river is a secure feeling to me now. The water takes me downstream with it, and knowing that I am moving keeps me satisfied. The river now meanders as if it really enjoys its surroundings and wishes to proceed no farther. There are broad calm areas where the current does not show itself and still pondlike areas alternating with stretches of riffles. It is a back and forth pace, slow then faster, slow then faster. In the quickly moving current, I laugh and delight in the way the stones on the river bottom speed by. I know how fast I am going compared with the slow, creeping, almost motionless pools. After sitting patiently in a pool as the ebb gradually takes me, or after paddling furiously and impatiently to get through the water past this pool into a riffle, the brisk feeling of moving in a riffle enlivens me.

The rain comes early with a bit of fog and a spray of drops. It sprinkles as the clouds lower and cover the hilltops. I don my poncho and listen for the tiny gatherings of moisture that touch down on my slick covering. The rain is upon everything, and the crystal clear sheen it lays upon the earth beads into drops and is smoothed into sheets that spread across surfaces. The moisture is dripping from the edges of my poncho, and when I hold my face to the sky to feel the force of falling drops, then look ahead again, I feel the moisture collecting in little spheres that drip from my nose and chin. The drops move across my face and tickle me with their gentle touch. I wonder if the drops tickle foliage and stone as much as they do me. All that is sensitive to tenderness and to minute pressure changes is stimulated now by the sliding roll of amoeba-like drops.

The rain fades, the air cools, and breeze slaps the wet surfaces of my face. The sky lifts a thousand feet, and hills are in view again. I think for a minute that I can see a patch of blue sky, but I know it is a combination of light gray and my great desire to see blue that causes these visions. I put on all the clothing I have—wool sweater, wool shirt, down vest, coat, and poncho, and still do not feel warm. A breeze can always find its way to my spine, which relays its shivering pulses.

The sky mists again, the ceiling dropping as great tongues of clouds drop out of the sky. They descend lower and lower as their weight of water is pulled to earth. All views are ended. I can see only a little shoebox-sized part of the valley—the section of river I am on, the bank on either side, and the ribbon of tall trees that grows at streamside. The day is continually cooling. Dampness snuffs any hopes of heat from the sun this day. I sit, watching wet miles and the wrinkles on my wet fingers.

I come upon a little slough that leads toward an old oxbow lake. I paddle *Blueberry* to the shore, tie up to a large rock, grab my fishing pole, and sneak to the still water. I expect to find pike in the slough, resting on the muddy bottom after a long evening and morning of the hunt. Where the slough meets the river, in a deep spot, I see my pike. I crouch down immediately and sneak closer to the water. I strip out fifteen feet of line and toss it into the area where the fish lies. I pull the line in a jerking manner to give some action to the lure, and the pike hits it like a rocket. With the force of its attack still welling up inside, it starts on a series of runs, jumps, head and body flailings, and displays of strength that almost rip the rod from my hand. But soon it tires. It is another sprinter pike, another ferocious whopper of a fish to dress up my dinner this evening. I hop back onto the raft and slide away into the silent miles of the Alatna.

My world is small now, a shrunken portion of the grand landscape I have viewed all the days of my travels. I cannot see beyond the trees of the riverbank. I feel as if I am floating in a dish of water, and there is no more to the world. All else is a cloud, a cool breath of sky that lets only diffuse light into my arena of life. I shiver off and on. I am chilled by the cold Alatna water at my feet and the settling drops surrounding my form. These are pristine moments. There is no wind, no waves on the water, and the fog blurs all else into a smear, into the notion that nothing else exists.

Soon it starts to rain harder, and after seven long, hard days of riding this raft on this river, I decide to take to shelter. I head toward the riverside and an open spruce stand where I tie up to a tree and hike into the forest to see if there is a level place to lie down. There sure is, and everywhere are little bushes bending under the great weight of wet blueberries. I set up my tent and as I work, I am visited by two mew gulls. They are white and opaque against the cluttered gray sky, and make innumerable passes by me, calling to each other and squawking at me in high tones. Back and forth they pass, squawking, landing in the trees, screaming at me. They are obviously disturbed by my presence, and I am sure they have a nest near here. I move my pack up to the camp and start a fire. There is plenty of dry kindling on the spruce, as the broad canopy catches the rain and the lower branches are dry. The gulls continue screaming at me with every pass overhead, and it seems as if they will go on forever. "Get out of here," I scream, and run to the river and throw rocks into the air. I know I could never hit them, so I laugh and try to ignore their noises, hoping at least they will silence later on so that I can sleep.

I sit out in the rain, and the smoke of the damp fire wafts around the area and hangs over the river. It mingles with the cool, damp air and settles in my hair and on my wool, and the wind waits to toss it about. I let the fire burn down, not adding new fuel. The coals glow for a moment, and the sizzling of drops striking the heat is the only sound I hear. The cooling water turns the fire to ash, powdery as the sky, and soon it is out. The sizzling stops, and the constant sound of drops dripping upon the shrubs and ground around me fills my ears. I can watch leaves snap back after being struck.

I crawl into my poncho-covered spot of earth, shake out my wool shirt, and lay it next to me. The smell of wet smoke has permeated all my damp clothing and perfumes the cool air.

Fireweed (*Epilobium angustifolium*)

August 8

The rain is on my roof all night. It is the same old song that has serenaded humans to sleep for as long as we have been on earth. It is soft staccato, continuous rhythms that echo in my nylon-enclosed cave. Drops splatter on the wet forest floor near my head, but I am dry, warm, and sparked by the sounds. I sleep the long hours of night and morning, and wake to the green growth of summer shrubs and sedges. Clouds are dripping onto the trees, trees are dripping onto my tent, and the ground eventually receives its drops.

I pull my head out of my sleeping bag and tent and look up toward the treetops. They are swaying in unison, back and forth with each gust of wind. The day is cold and it appears that it may rain for quite a while. A wind gathers up the wet cold and rams it through me. Floating on the river will be chilling.

I eat granola in my shelter and dream of other places. I wonder what primitive man would have done on days like this when he had food and did not have to travel or mend something. I dream of the many days of this trip, of the hardships, of being alone, of the moments when, as now, I think instead of speak, and look at trees and drops of moisture on green leaves instead of into another pair of human eyes. Life these long hours is filled with waiting and dreaming. I dream of the country I have seen and lived with; I dream of wanting to share my thoughts with another person; and indeed now, I speak my mind, wordlessly, pouring out to a fictitious face, to a woman's heart I need in these lonely times.

I sleep on and off through the morning, dreaming heavily, waking again and again. My normal rhythm of waking has been disrupted by sleeping these extra hours, and I feel disoriented with each reawakening. The rain comes hard, with winds that billow my flimsy shelter. It does not make me feel like crawling from my sleeping bag. I can feel the chill without even being outside. I sleep some more, fill my journal with worded memories of rafting, waiting, and wanting, then try to read a bit. But I cannot read today. I cannot concentrate on fantasy, on other dream events, when my mind, my forces, and the things that surround me are so real and demand all my attention now. I roll over and over, and finally put on my clothing and boots, throw my gear together, tie it onto *Blueberry*, and shove off into the weather, into the mainstream of river life.

The water moves slowly and takes me slowly, creeping at a walking pace along its winding course. The wind shuffles through my beard and works its way down my neck. I shiver, expel the arm of wind, and hunch my shoulders up and my neck down to fill the space in my collar and keep the warmth in and the wind out. I lay a pole across my lap because a gentle paddle is occasionally necessary to keep my direction. I float down a long, straight stretch of river with a hill running on both sides. Dwarfed black spruce (many of which are burned) cover the hill to the south. Fireweed flares the hills with pink blossoms and draws life from the gray sky with the simple addition of color.

On a long, slow bend, I see some animals on the sandy shore of the river. They are quite a way ahead, and I hope I can get to see them closer before they become scared, and vanish into the forest. As I float closer, I see that they are red fox pups, three of them, frolicking in the drizzle. They jump on each other, biting and rolling and playing like puppy dogs. All of a sudden, they see me and stop. They look curiously at me, then scamper to the riverside and sit up, all three in a row. They twist their heads to each side, sizing me up, sniffing at me. Their mother lounges in the grass at the forest's edge. She is looking at me, unconcerned. I continue downstream, and the mother stands up, stretches, runs parallel to the route that I follow, then darts off into the forest. The pups run alongside the river, barking at me, and occasionally stopping to play and jump on each other. I feel like poling to shore and picking up a pup to take with me, but know that these animals belong here. They frolic alongside, then stop, and I soon lose sight of them against the continuous shore and endless trees of the riverside.

I find another pike in an intermittent stream channel and bring him along for dinner. The cold comes and goes, as the wind comes and goes. When I saw the foxes or caught the pike, despite whether the wind was blowing or it was calm, I was warm. The excitement and concentration that were generated kept any chill far away. Now, sitting looking upon gray skies and wet forests hazed over by rain, there is nothing I can do to be warm. A few short-lived thoughts warm me, but the wind quickly blows them away, and I return to the chill, to here and now.

I follow a deep narrow channel that cuts against the hillside and has steep sides. Numerous eddies swirl behind rocks or deeper-cut areas of the hillside. I pole along the bank, pushing to keep myself in the middle of the channel. There are some swift riffles, which raises a laugh in me, and then the channels merge and flow around a bend where the water is deep and clear and the river shows all its small stones. On the map, I see this is the location of Oscar's cabin, but I do not see any cabin. It must have been built long ago and now it has fallen down, caved in by winter snows and grown over with mosses.

Rain, rain, rain. I lie reading and reading and reading. I become enthralled with the fantasy of Tolkien's trilogy, but again think it is ridiculous to read here. Back and forth my mind wavers between the reality of the rainy valley and the enjoyment that escaping into a book brings. I roll onto one side, taking turns holding the book with one hand then the other. The holding hand is out away from the rest of my body and quickly loses its heat, becoming numbed. As I switch hands, I put the cold one under an armpit, and by the time the holding hand is cold, the warming hand is warm. Back and forth I shift hands, until both hands are tired and regain heat slowly, and neither hand can last one page.

I roll onto my back, snuggle down into my bag, and tuck both hands deep into my armpits. I shiver a few times, long pulsating tremors that push the goose bumps (and the cold) from my scalp. The sleeping bag billows with warmth — my own little environment, under a rain poncho, away from the weather. How cozy and secure it feels to inhabit the only warm spot in all these miles. But still my back hurts.

I wonder what I am doing here, nestling uncomfortably in my cozy shelter. I am escaping the rain and wind and cold air, but I also am just lying here. I need to be out, to see more of this country, to see the river's end. The rain is hard upon my roof. I hold my breath to hear each drop strike the nylon. In my tent, hundreds of mosquitoes take refuge. They are chilled and do not bother me a bit. At the peak where my willow poles hold things upright, they sit next to one another, almost coating the material with their bodies. It is tempting to strike and kill as many as I can, but they are not bothering me, and I am amused at how they deal with one another — landing upon each other, pushing their way through crowds, standing on their four front legs with their rear legs straight out behind them. They bend their legs at the joints, working them back and forth as if they were stiff and the activity might loosen them up. They remind me of sprinters in starting blocks, and I laugh at comparing insects that I hate (mosquitoes) to animals that I love (people). How desperate I must be for company.

The rain beats down, then slackens into a soft drizzle, becoming light, then lighter. Do I want to lie here or do I want to get with it? I pack my gear, put on all my clothing, with the poncho on top, and float away. The water is slow, but soon there is fine, swift water. I pass the spot where Black Jack cabin should be, but it, too, has apparently been broken down by time and weather.

I start into a series of curves, which will end where the Alatna meets the Koyukuk River. It is still a long way, beyond my reach for today. A fine mist settles everywhere, and I stop to pick blueberries. The area is open, with trees here and there, standing solitary above the birch and willow shrubs, with bushes of blueberries and Labrador tea below them. The picking is good, and I love tramping across thick, saturated, spongelike moss mats and soggy shrubs and ground looking for blueberries. I collect a small bagful and head off again downstream.

The rain is almost foglike, obscuring distant objects. I think I see a small aluminum boat with a motor up ahead, tied to a gravelly shore. I am apprehensive about seeing more people. Coming closer, I see there are salmon drying under a wooden roof, and the smell of fish fills the air.

I pole over to shore, drag *Blueberry* up on the gravel, and walk up the path toward the small log cabin. As I come closer, I see a man in the window. He looks up from his work, then looks down, then his head jerks up again. He drops what he's doing and comes out the door to meet me. Bob McGuire is his name, and I introduce myself. "Rainy day," I say, and we go into the cabin. The door is built so low that I have to bend down to get in. In the winter, a cabin stays warmer if the door is as low as possible, because heat rises to escape through the joints around the door. The inside of the cabin is made of peeled logs, fresh and exquisite. The room has a table by the front window, a barrel stove, a shelf with supplies, a bed in one corner, and little else. Bob's wife, Cora, a young baby, and an older child are also in the cabin. Cora fixes a round of tea, and I take off my poncho and hang it on the door. Bob asks me where I have come from and I tell him. He looks at me seriously and says, "That's a long way to come alone." He doesn't seem so surprised to hear that I have come that far — in the old days, travel was always overland like that. But no one would travel alone. It was too dangerous, too easy to get hurt or lost, and either circumstance could mean death in a big country like the Brooks Range. I tell him I have carried all my dry food, caught grayling and pike, and dug roots and collected leaves and berries. He shakes his head, wondering how I have carried what I have over all those miles.

I ask how fishing is, and he tells me they have not been fishing real hard. Setting gill nets in eddies, they catch salmon that are migrating upstream, but the fish are less common than ever. He blames it on the "big boats" that are fishing out in the ocean and "catching them all before they can get in the river." I wonder whether it is just a bad year, but I don't ask. They use the fish mainly for dog food. It is pretty appalling to think of that good meat going to feed dogs, but dogs provide winter transportation in Alaska and so they must be fed well. Temperatures here can get low — minus seventy degrees Fahrenheit — and dogs that sleep and work outside require a rich diet with lots of fats.

Caribou are scarce these days, too, Bob says, but he does not depend on caribou. Instead, he eats moose, which are getting less and less common. I tell him I have found lots of grayling, pike, vegetables, and berries, but such trivial things do not matter when a native is talking about a few caribou, a couple of moose, or hundreds of salmon. Here, food for the winter and spring means great quantities of food. "There's a lot of old boys who depend on moose for their livelihood. What's going to happen to them in the future? Where else can you go after you've lived in Alaska?"

Where else, indeed. This is the end of the last road into the real wilderness. And it is being overused by takers who have nothing to give back. A land can support only so many consumers. Competition between natives and newcomers (and natives who have been influenced by them) now is reducing the richness of wild Alaska. Modern, "civilized" ways and a disregard for preserving finite resources are making it harder and harder to live as native Alaskans have for generations. It frightens me to think that this is the end of a world—a small corner of a primitive world where people can still live with the land, finding all they need for their physical and spiritual sustenance. If only there were a way to leave it all alone, or to let natives live on it and with it as they always have, with other human beings allowed only to visit but not compete for the resources.

I leave the cabin on a solemn note. The McGuires walk out with me into the clouded world. Everything is calm, not a breath of wind moves a branch or leaf. A drizzle has just ended, and we stand for a second, together on the riverbank. As I push the raft out onto the river, I turn to say good-bye. Bob holds up his arm and says "*Kon-Tiki*, away." "Good-bye," I say. "Good-bye."

They turn and go back to their cabin as I paddle out into the middle of the Alatna. The rain comes down again. I am surrounded by the sounds of drops on water, and the motion of the river sweeping me downstream. Shivers run up my spine again, for the thousandth time since Anaktuvuk Pass. I feel how the greatness of this land dangles on some fragile pendulum, the balance of natives and newcomers being broken down further and further each year.

I think of things that I have taken from this land, as my shadow, my footsteps, my mind have passed the miles of valleys that again rest unseen. I have taken some food, some water, some wood, some pleasure. And what have I given back but my sweat, curses, tears, wastes, and expressions of infinite joy? What can I give to this country but my understanding of it to other interested people so that they might help it remain wild?

The land is by nature in balance. The natives live with nature and so partly become one with it. Only the newcomers take the balance away through their ignorance and disrespect.

I do not go far this day. I float around another bend or so and then settle back into the forest, into the wet land, to ponder the many paths I have taken and can take in the days to come.

Red fox

It isn't raining this morning. The clouds are high, and I am floating on the river very early, eagerly anticipating this last batch of bends! The current here is better than I had expected, and I am moving along without complaint. I feel as if I could make it to Allakaket today, but I know from Bob that today is Tuesday, and the mail plane comes in around noon. I never could make it. There is no reason to get there tonight either, so I may as well relax and get there tomorrow night, enjoying the last days and miles of this trip. I can catch the Thursday mail plane.

The clouds part and the sun shows through. At first sight I close my eyes and point my face into the sun. Ah, what warm feelings. How easy it is to forget this feeling of sun and bright light upon leaves and water. I peel off layers of wool and down, until I sit in my cotton T-shirt, hugging the warm air that engulfs me.

I stop to pick blueberries. I wander around on my knees, filling my hat with handfuls of berries. Each time I look up, I reorient myself to where the river is. I lie back for awhile and leisurely drop blueberries into my waiting mouth. Isn't this the life? Insects are scarce, the sun is out and seems brand new, and everything is still fresh from the past day's rains. I hear a droning in the distance to the south. A motor boat is coming up the river. I do not want to meet more people, yet I realize that I am within thirty miles of Allakaket and people use these waterways as highways. The boat seems to take an awfully long time to reach here, but I know how much the river meanders and how many river miles it takes to get a few air miles. I crawl to the forest's edge to watch them pass. One man, one woman, one long, slender boat. They move fast on the water, and I wonder whether the wake will disturb my raft's position on the bank. I look up and down the riverside, but no raft! I panic. My heart pounds. I drop my blueberries and run downriver along the shore. I have no idea when it floated away or how far it has gone. I talk myself into believing that I can run as fast as it can float, and then I can swim out to meet it. Oh, what crazy ideas. I could never catch it. I can visualize the raft floating downstream past the village this evening, with no rider. Everyone will wonder what is going on. I know someone will motor out and tow the raft home and delight in finding my gear. All I have got here is what I have on—no warm clothing, no anything. This is a miserable way to spend the last days of my trip.

But before the thoughts have emerged as screams or tears, I see *Blueberry* up ahead a few hundred yards. I cannot believe it. The natives must have tied it to shore when they discovered it. I wonder whether anything has fallen off or whether they have taken anything. Oh, who cares? My raft is safe, and I am intact again. I run as fast as I can to touch it, laughing and shouting. It is tied to a tree, and everything is just as I had left it.

I hike back upriver to find my blueberry-filled hat. It's funny how I never think about certain things until unusual events remind me. Of all the hours on the river, my raft floats away now, at precisely the same moment that this boat comes by to rescue it. There is a one in a million chance that these two events could happen at the same time. Is it by luck or good fortune that this happens to me here? Is there something or someone watching over me that stepped in and provided these circumstances?

I float down the river for awhile to calm myself, and soon stop again for more blueberries. This time, I tie the raft to a tree. I will take no more chances. I collect another bag of berries and decide to stay for awhile and write. I build a small fire and prepare a blueberry pie as usual. Then I put several marble-sized pieces of gravel in my pot and place the pie on top of them. It makes my pot more oven-like. I take three willows and lean them together at the top. From the peak, I hang my pot by the handle so that it is about five or six inches above the coals. I write while the berries boil, and then cool in their new form—blueberry pie for a midafternoon snack. They say man cannot live by bread alone, but they don't say that about blueberries!

I get back on the river. Clouds build up again in a small cluster overhead. The sun is hidden and a shower pours down. A raindrop hits the water, forms a ring, rebounds about a half inch, and lies on the surface as a skittering silver bead. Then, poof, it pops and disappears. I see thousands of these at any instant and billions are on the river. It is a dazzling spectacle. Up ahead, four loons are on the water. They swim with the current, warily keeping about a hundred yards ahead. They talk to each other and screech in voices that remind me of children.

Belted kingfishers also are common on the banks. They are large, blue, crested birds, and I occasionally see them dive headfirst into the river for small fish. They have a rapid chattering call that is unmistakable, and fly on the power of quick wingbeats interspersed with seconds of sailing. They are grand to watch, and for a second, I wish I could be a bird and fly at any height I chose above the river. This thought is dispelled as I remember how small the brain of a bird is. I would rather have my brain and be plagued with a clumsy, earthbound body.

I stop in an ideal place for the remainder of the afternoon and evening. The forest is open and the ground dry. The blueberries here look like the best of any I have seen yet. Blueberry madness sets in, in full force. I am crazed with picking attacks. I almost cannot control it. I pick a bush clean, and another and another, and think to myself, "This is enough." But I pick another bush and there's another right next to it, and the bushes cover the forest floor and seemingly go on this way over the hill and off into the distant sunset. Endless berries. I have met my match. I cannot pick them all.

It is so hard to conceptualize the passing of five weeks' time. It is so difficult to save all the memories so they will always stay with me. This trip started so hard, but also so easy. An idea was born sometime in the winter, blossomed into preparation, grew and became what I wanted.

Now I am living the experience. It is me, and I am an expression of the nature of this land. When I walk away, it will be gone from me. No more backbreaking hikes through endless miles of tussocks and hummocks. No more swarms of mosquitoes. No more dense thickets of alders. No more long days adrift on the sleepy Alatna. It is easy to think about leaving these things because now I remember the grueling, painful minutes. But such times are true reflections of the nature of this wild and rigorous country. It is a long, long way between two villages, and surviving in the Brooks Range is an expression of a person's ability to live naturally, simply, wisely with the land.

The things I have experienced and am still experiencing are things the way they really are. I could fly over the miles or speed through many of them in a motor boat, but that isn't what this country is about. It's one-step-after-the-other country; it's fully living each and every move between tussocks, planning routes a hundred yards at a time day after day, following streams to their sources, seeing every inch of channels, crossing divides, and following rivers from their first trickling origins. I have sweated and complained and cursed at the hardships. I have cried from the pain of being alone during all the trials the land has put me through. Still, somewhere inside me I have found the strength to go on, to live and see another day as man has always done. I feel primitive and entirely myself here, living with this land on its own terms, without machines, without the aid of anyone else, being entirely on my own as I make my own way, my own life. The life-forms, colors, endless walking in pristine country fill me with incredible satisfaction. Everything in this country is on earth for simple reasons. I understand the harmony, the order in the complex communities of nature, and living with these native species has helped me understand the riches to which they cling. This all has inspired me and provided everything I have needed to survive here. I love it, or I would have left or died long ago.

I am close to completing my long journey—I can taste it and feel it inside me. I take a long look around me, my last home in the wilderness. I scan the shrubs and community of life that calls this their permanent home. The tall willows, the bearberries and blueberries, the carpets of mosses are all forms that are indigenous to this country. I have come to know them well and feel at one with this wilderness.

Having absorbed as much as I can, I grab all my gear, tie it onto *Blueberry*, and paddle out into the current. These logs and I finally seem to understand each other and respond to the river perfectly. We float flawlessly, negotiating each bend, curve, and speedway with ease.

The day is warm—summer again. I feel as if I am out of the mountains for the first time in a long, long while, out on the flatlands where I can see great distances. The sky is a maze of thunderheads and blue holes between clouds. The billowy whites are blended and frayed; the grays, blacks, and blues were never truer colors. Veils of clouds are shrouded everywhere. Rain in the distance streaks across the sky in curved, combed patterns. I can look straight up along the sides of thunderheads and almost feel the endlessly detailed curves and textures of these masses of moisture.

Bend after bend I float through, mile after mile. I enjoy each minute, knowing that I have come the length of this river, from the source of one of its major tributaries, the Kutuk. I have seen the moods and ways a river works. I study the map as I have the whole trip, noting each meander and the characteristics of country at each one. The river makes one last horseshoe heading east, then west, and finally south. Rounding the last bend, I anticipate seeing the end of the Alatna. My heart beats faster, my knees shake. Then perhaps a half mile ahead, I see it — the Koyukuk River, the river into which the Alatna spills its blood, its produce. I stand up, anxious with anticipation. It has been such a long journey and only for one second am I able to experience the feeling of, "Ah, I have made it." I realize the Koyukuk is a wide river. Will I be able to paddle across it?

I hear a motor boat coming down the Alatna and here, in this last stretch, come Bob, Cora, and the two children. They pull up alongside and float with me. He says, "I saw the biggest grizzly bear I've ever seen a few miles upriver from the cabin the day after we saw you." His description makes it sound like the area I had camped in the night before I saw them. I feel as if I look pale. Then I laugh and say, "No, I didn't see him. He must have been afraid to come around when I was there." We smile, exchange a few more bits of information, and then they motor off.

I can hardly sit. I float closer, closer, closer, and I see the river right before me. Then we mingle. "Alatna meet Koyukuk." It is a swift-moving, strong, muddy river, swollen with the week's rains. Though I am still not sure that I can paddle across it, I grit my teeth and start paddling in strong, deep strokes, alternating sides. I can see Allakaket across the river downstream about a quarter mile or so and the village of Alatna on the same side of the river where the Alatna comes in.

I see the big house where I want to land the raft, and I paddle furiously across the river, paddling hard again and again. And finally I do it! I reach the opposite bank, jump off with my front rope in hand, and drag *Blueberry* up onto the shore. I smile the deepest smile of my life and stand there glassy eyed, looking back up toward the Alatna Hills, and toward the Brooks Range, which is out of sight beyond them. I feel dazed. I am here, Allakaket, at long last.

People are looking at me from the riverbank. Children come up to me asking how have my logs stayed together, what did I shoot with my bow, and endless other questions. I take my pack off *Blueberry*, cut the lashings, and drag the logs onto shore and give them away. I hoist my pack and walk into the village. It consists of twenty to thirty log homes, a mission dating from the early part of the century, and a boardwalk through town. There are no cars, few fancy items, but lots of fuel barrels for motor boats that line the river, and snowmobiles.

One old fellow dressed in western clothing is standing on his front porch, chewing on a bone. He stares at me as I walk up. Then he smiles and says, "You don't look like you're from around here." I smile back and tell him where I've come from. He says people used to travel like that—ninety-eighters, prospectors—but people just do not do that anymore. He tells me where the store is, as I need to buy a few things. The doors and windows in all the homes are open. No rooms are within them—just one big room for everyone. Nothing to hide.

The store is in someone's home, on one wall of their kitchen area. They have a few boxes of cake mix, soap, potatoes, onions, a slab of bacon—that's about it. The prices are unreasonable, or so I guess, but I don't ask. I don't care.

Back on the streets, kids follow me. Teenage girls in jeans go by, shy and giggling just like teenage girls everywhere. I hike through the village to the river and set up camp on the shore. I cook chunks of bacon on my grill and boil two potatoes and one onion. All the local wood is wet, and so I split alder branches lengthwise to keep my fire burning. It keeps me busy. The bacon drips with fat and the potful of boiled tubers looks inviting. I eat the huge feast and can hardly get it all down. I feel like a python who is trying to swallow a cow, and already has it halfway down before realizing it is a cow. My stomach is so full and stretched that it is uncomfortable to breathe. I cannot walk, or even smile, but thinking about how funny this is, I start laughing and immediately lose the whole works.

The bluffs across the river, behind the village of Alatna, are covered with birches and poplars, yellow green in the light of the setting sun. The sky turns orange with painted clouds. The breeze is up, the gnats and mosquitoes almost gone. I think back on my journey and how, out of the thirty-six days, I have seen rain on perhaps twenty-five of them, but have not glimpsed a rainbow. It has been a great disappointment. But when I landed *Blueberry* for the last time, a sprinkle of rain fell on the land from a far-off cloud mass. It stirred up clouds of gnats and the fellow helping me ran inside. As the cloud of insects and rain cleared, I saw an amazing sight. There before my eyes appeared not one but two huge rainbows sparkling across the sky.

Selected Reading

Brower, Kenneth. *Earth and the Great Weather: The Brooks Range.* New York: Friends of the Earth, 1971.

Crisler, Lois. *Arctic Wild.* New York: Harper & Row, 1973.

Helmericks, Constance and Harmon. *The Flight of the Arctic Tern.* New York: Little, Brown & Company, 1952.

Marshall, Robert. *Alaska Wilderness: Exploring the Central Brooks Range.* Berkeley: University of California Press, 1956.

————. *Arctic Village.* New York: The Literary Guild, 1933.

Milton, John P. *Nameless Valleys, Shining Mountains: The Record of an Expedition into the Vanishing Wilderness of Alaska's Brooks Range.* New York: Walker, 1970.

Murie, Margaret E. *Two in the Far North.* New York: Alfred A. Knopf, 1957.